COME
HOLY SPIRIT
RENEW THE WHOLE CREATION

SIX BIBLE STUDIES

On the Theme of the
Seventh Assembly
of the
World Council of Churches

ƒ

FRIENDSHIP PRESS • NEW YORK

United States of America Edition by Friendship Press

Editorial Office: 475 Riverside Drive (772)
                   New York, NY 10115

Distribution Office: PO Box 37844
                      Cincinnati, OH 45222-0844

Design: Edwin Hassink/WCC

ISBN 0-377-00203-8

© 1989 WCC Publications, World Council of Churches,
150, route de Ferney, P.O. Box 2100, 1211 Geneva 2, Switzerland

Printed in United States of America

Library of Congress Cataloging-in-Publication Data
Come, Holy Spirit, renew the whole creation: six Bible studies: on the theme
  of the Seventh Assembly of the World Council of Churches. — North
  American ed.
        p.   cm.
    Includes bibliographical references.
    ISBN 0-377-00203-8: $4.95
    1. Holy Spirit—Biblical teaching. 2. Bible—Study. I. World
Council of Churches. Assembly (7th: 1991: Canberra, A.C.T.)
BS680.H56C66   1989
231′.3—dc20   89-27297
                                                             CIP

Contents

Come Holy Spirit
Renew the Whole Creation

Dear Friends,

This volume of six Bible studies related to the theme of the Seventh Assembly of the World Council of Churches is an extraordinary gift and invitation.

We receive the gift from Christian sisters and brothers from around the world in the form of their testimonies and comments on selected passages of Scripture. Through their sharing we can feel and experience the meaning of Christian community.

The invitation comes to each of us—wherever we may be—to join with others in opening ourselves to the Holy Spirit and to a fresh understanding of how the Bible "speaks" to us today. These studies provide an exciting opportunity for us to join hearts and hopes with millions of other Christians who yearn for renewal.

These Bible studies are a very significant way in which those of us who live in Canada and the United States can participate in the great Assembly that will take place in Canberra, Australia. Not many of us will actually be at that meeting. Yet we recall how the Sixth Assembly in Vancouver, Canada, refreshed our spirits. Therefore, as we study these texts let us pray for those who meet in Canberra; let us, with them, ask the Spirit of Unity to reconcile God's people.

James A. Hamilton
General Secretary
National Council of the
Churches of Christ in the U.S.A.

An Invitation to Bible Study

Dear Friends,

The Seventh Assembly of the World Council of Churches will be held in Canberra, Australia, in February 1991. The theme chosen for the Assembly is the prayer: "Come, Holy Spirit — Renew the Whole Creation."

Not all of us can be physically present in Canberra, but we can all participate in the Assembly in spirit and in prayer. One of the most meaningful ways of sharing in this ecumenical pilgrimage is through the study of the Bible. Bible study will be central to the life of the Assembly, as it is central to the life of the World Council.

The six studies presented in this booklet are meant for groups of Christian people in all parts of the world. We invite you to join this spiritual journey as an act of ecumenical solidarity and as an expression of our common Christian commitment.

Emilio Castro
General Secretary
World Council of Churches
Geneva

Introduction

The World Council of Churches

The World Council of Churches, says the Basis to which each of its member churches subscribes, is "a fellowship of churches which confess the Lord Jesus Christ as God and Saviour according to the Scriptures and therefore seek to fulfill together their common calling to the glory of the one God, Father, Son and Holy Spirit".

The vision of church unity was never completely lost during the many centuries of schism and conflict among Christians. In the late nineteenth century, however, the conviction began to take hold in several places that something must be done to heal the divisions which have always hampered Christian witness. That marked the beginning of the modern ecumenical movement in which the unique fellowship of the WCC is rooted.

In particular, the ecumenical movement owes its origin to missionaries and Sunday school workers, young people and university students from many different Christian traditions who began meeting and praying and planning together across denominational lines.

An ecumenical vision was taking form — the daring vision of a fellowship that could make real the prayer of Jesus "that they may all be one... that the world might believe".

Following a world missionary conference in Edinburgh, Scotland, in 1910, the drive towards unity began to take organizational shape. Three related movements were founded in the 1920s. The International Missionary Council (1921) brought together foreign missionary societies and national Christian councils for study and common action on Christian witness. The Life and Work movement (1925) explored Christian responsibility in the face of urgent social issues. The Faith and Order movement (1927) confronted the thorny controversies and differences over doctrine and authority which often lead to and strengthen church divisions.

Meanwhile, the Ecumenical Patriarchate of Constantinople, emerging at the end of the first world war from centuries of isolation under the Ottoman Empire, was turning its eyes outward to other Christian churches. An encyclical letter, sent by the synod of this church in 1920 "to all the churches of Christ everywhere", called for a "league of churches" to be formed. It was the first official ecclesiastical proposal for an institutional expression of worldwide ecumenism. In the decades to come, Orthodox church leaders played an active role in Faith and Order, Life and Work, the International Missionary Council and in ecumenical student movements.

In 1937 church leaders decided that the time was ripe to merge the Faith and Order and Life and Work movements into a World Council of Churches. The outbreak of the second world war delayed the implementation of that decision for eleven years — until August 1948, when representatives of 147 churches met to constitute the WCC at its First Assembly in Amsterdam. Although several Orthodox churches decided against joining the WCC in 1948, ecumenical contact with them continued, and after the Third Assembly (New Delhi, 1961) all of the Orthodox churches in the world had become WCC members.

The International Missionary Council continued to exist independently, though in close cooperation with the WCC, until 1961. The concerns which motivated these three movements, as well as those of the World Council of Christian Education, which merged with the WCC in 1971, remain at the centre of the Council's agenda today.

Most of the 147 churches that came to Amsterdam in 1948 were European or North American. Since then, the number of member churches has more than doubled (it now stands at 306); and the Council has increasingly become a world body. Churches from Africa, Asia, the Caribbean, Latin America, the Middle East and the Pacific have become a vital part of the ecumenical fellowship.

Many of these churches have a long history, but the WCC membership also includes "younger" Pentecostal bodies and Independent churches in Africa and Asia. Successful union negotiations have sometimes replaced two or more previous member churches with one united denomination. At the same time, women, lay people and youth have taken an increasing role in WCC leadership.

Although the Roman Catholic Church is not a member of the WCC, it works together ecumenically with the Council in several important ways.

A Joint Working Group oversees five areas of cooperation — the way towards unity, common witness, social collaboration, ecumenical formation and ongoing cooperation between the Roman Catholic Church and several WCC commissions.

As an instrument of the one ecumenical movement, the WCC works together with many partner organizations — national councils and regional conferences of churches, confessional bodies and other ecumenical groups. The WCC claims no authority to legislate for its member churches; but each member of this fellowship of churches has pledged to search together with the others for ways to express visible unity and obedience.

That involves common encounter, theological study, witness and service. To respond, through relevant programmes, to the challenges the churches have asked it to face, the WCC maintains a staff of about 300 people at its headquarters in Geneva, Switzerland. This staff is divided into three programme units — Faith and Witness, Justice and Service, Education and Renewal, whose various sub-units study, consult and act — and a General Secretariat which includes administrative offices whose work has to do with the entire Council.

The Seventh Assembly

Canberra, Australia: 7-20 February 1991

For the seventh time since its inauguration in Amsterdam, member churches of the WCC will meet in assembly. From all over the world delegates will come to Canberra, the federal capital of Australia, to meet one another, to take counsel together and "to listen to what the Spirit is saying to the churches".

Each assembly is an occasion for the churches to renew their commitment in the light of the challenges they face. In Canberra they will do this in the words of the prayer which is the theme of the assembly: "Come Holy Spirit — Renew the Whole Creation".

Who will be there? Around 950 official delegates of the member churches will be joined by an equal number of representatives of other churches and organizations, advisers, guests, observers, staff and stewards. There will also be a full complement of visitors and members of the press. No

more diverse or representative a Christian gathering is likely to take place anywhere in the world at the present time!

What will they do? The theme will permeate the entire life of the assembly — its celebrations, its deliberations and its decision-making.

Through worship the churches will reaffirm the covenant they have made with one another in the WCC. Participants will celebrate the unity Christians already share and their common life as God's people. In prayer and Bible study, the assembly will meditate on the theme and seek a deeper awareness of the power of the Holy Spirit at work in our lives and in our world.

In its deliberations the assembly will probe the theological meaning of the theme, the sub-themes and the issues that arise from them which are pertinent to the life and work of the WCC. As the highest constitutional decision-making body of the WCC, the assembly has the responsibility of electing from among the delegates the members of the Central Committee, as well as the members of the Presidium, who will oversee and direct the work of the Council until the next assembly. It will also receive and act on proposals related to programme, public responsibility and other concerns, and may also make its own recommendations to the member churches or the Central Committee.

What issues will be on the agenda? The work of an assembly is at the same time the culmination of the WCC's work since the last assembly and the starting point for its work until the next assembly.

The Sixth Assembly in Vancouver 1983 gave the WCC several guidelines to "inspire all WCC activities in the coming years". The Council was charged in all its work to seek growth — growth towards unity, towards justice and peace, towards a vital and coherent theology, towards new dimensions of the churches' self-understanding, towards a community of confessing and learning. The assembly also identified other areas of work, such as a process of mutual commitment to justice, peace and the integrity of creation, the concerns and perspectives of women, and ecumenical learning.

All these will be reflected in the report of the Council's work, *Vancouver to Canberra,* to be published early in 1990. It will be the task of the Canberra Assembly, in the light of this report, to give new directions for the future work of the Council. The exploration of the theme and sub-themes, as well as other presentations, will enable the assembly to discern the issues and priorities which should guide the work of the WCC until the next assembly.

What will be the programme of the assembly? The assembly will begin each day with a common act of worship, and throughout the assembly participants will engage in various forms of liturgical celebration, special observances and acts of commitment. There will be several different forms of gathering and working: plenary sessions for special presentations or official business; four sections for study of the sub-themes and consideration of issues; smaller groups for Bible study or other discussions. A special programme for visitors will enable them to hear assembly speakers and learn more about the ecumenical movement and the WCC.

How can we be involved in the assembly? Although only a limited number of people can actually attend the assembly, we can all share in various ways. For example we can:
— Arrange meetings with delegates or other participants before or after the assembly.
— Gather as groups to share in the Bible studies in this booklet and also to discuss the issues that will be considered by the assembly.
— Use the *Ecumenical Prayer Cycle* in our church, prayer group or privately, and pray for other churches and Christians, and become familiar with the rich diversity of Christians who make up the ecumenical fellowship.

Those interested in attending the assembly as visitors should write to the WCC Assembly Office in Geneva or (for US citizens) the WCC office in New York or (for Australians) the WCC Assembly Office in Sydney.

The Theme and Sub-themes

The theme: Come, Holy Spirit — Renew the Whole Creation

The renewal of all life through God's pouring out the Spirit is one of the powerful images in the Old Testament. In the New Testament the outpouring of the Holy Spirit on the day of Pentecost is seen as the event that gathered the believers as a community of faith — the church. The first disciples experienced the Holy Spirit as the source of their faith, hope and joy and as the power at work among them. In course of time the church learned to confess the Spirit as "the Lord, the Giver of life".

Christian tradition affirms the Holy Spirit as the One who confirms believers in their faith. In the Spirit God comes to us in Jesus Christ, is with us and in us. Through the Spirit God sustains all creation, life and history. In the Spirit God is our advocate and comforter. Through the Spirit all faith, life and history are rooted in the life of God the Father, active and present in Jesus Christ.

The Spirit engenders and nourishes the faith of God's people through the proclamation of the gospel and the celebration of the sacraments. In the Spirit the community of believers experience the nearness of God and participate in the saving grace and the liberating presence of the living Christ, thus becoming the instrument and sign of God's transforming action.

The Spirit also calls us to repentance, for we, through our personal and corporate sin, have brought violence and destruction to the world. God's gifts in creation are meant to be shared. Instead we have tried to own them and to use them for our own ends. But the Spirit who exposes what is evil in the world also promises to give us a new life and to renew the whole creation.

The transformation that the Spirit brings restores our communion with God and one another. We are built up through the gifts of the Spirit into a people empowered to do God's will, to share the good news, and to become a community of sharing. We are carried beyond our narrow personal concerns to strive for justice and peace in the world and to be in solidarity with the poor and the oppressed. We are called to uphold and preserve the gift of God's creation. Indeed the Spirit lifts up our vision and points us to the renewal of the whole created order.

As we pray for this renewal, we seek to discern and participate in the activity of the Holy Spirit in all places where God's love is made manifest, in the hope of a world reconciled to God, a creation renewed according to God's will. And we do so with Christian people in all parts of the world, from vastly different cultures, traditions and situations as they too call upon the Holy Spirit and pray for the renewal of the whole world.

The sub-themes

Our prayer, like all prayers, is an act of commitment. The sub-themes are meant to explore the areas and concerns where our commitment must find expression. They provide the link between our confession of faith and the demands it makes on us in today's historical context. From our theological affirmations about the Holy Spirit emerge programmatic issues for the churches and the WCC. We pray; and as we pray we also ask: what would the Spirit have us do?

Sub-theme 1: *Giver of Life — Sustain your Creation!*

The life of the world can be sustained, preserved and made new only when it is accepted as God's creation and a gift of the Spirit. This world, the rich variety of its life, belongs to God. The church is empowered by the Spirit to confess this truth and to witness and work for sustaining the wholeness of creation.

This impels us to work with people and movements committed to cherish the earth and to resist those that work against life and plunder the earth. It helps us to uncover the violence that underlies so much of our attitude to creation and to one another. We look, therefore, with the guidance of the Spirit, for ways of living the biblical vision of a world reconciled in God. We try to discern the experience of indigenous peoples who have sought through the centuries to live in harmony with the rest of creation. We try to learn from other living faiths and their perspectives on creation, and from all who labour to nurture life in many ways.

This sub-theme will consider the theology of creation. It will involve identifying and confronting the forces that undermine the environmental foundations of life in our world today. It should lead us to giving serious attention to the ecological models of economic life which nurture the earth, the challenges presented by the depletion of species and resources, and the issues raised by genetic engineering and unhampered economic growth.

Sub-theme 2: *Spirit of Truth — Set us Free!*

The liberating witness of the Holy Spirit is most clearly seen in the life and ministry of Christ, a foretaste of the liberation that God intends for all creation. As part of the process of liberation, the Spirit exposes and convicts the world of sin — the sin that holds us "in bondage to slavery". And it is the Spirit of truth that leads us into the truth that makes us free.

We recognize the "principalities and powers" that oppose God's will for justice and peace on earth. They find expression in social and economic systems that divide humankind and perpetuate the deep divisions based

on race, religion, colour and sex, in political systems that escalate con-
flicts, in the arms race and in the violations of the rights of people.

It is out of this context of systematic injustice that the churches are chal-
lenged to join the powerless of the earth — the poor, the exploited and the
marginalized — and those who try to be with them as they seek truth and
freedom. We join them not as people without hope, for the same Spirit, the
Advocate who convinces the world of sin, also works with us and through
us as we struggle against injustice and to shake off the chains that bind us.
The Spirit makes available to us the resources that can help us in our
individual and corporate efforts to build life in community.

Through this sub-theme the assembly will try to discern the theological
basis of our search for justice and peace and of our common participation
with others in the service of humankind. It will try to clarify the question
of the church's own attitude to and participation in power. It will try to
discern the church's mission in the technological society responsible for
an economic system that creates the deepening debt crises of our times,
contributes to the rise of militarism and to the ecological crisis. It will
attempt to discover the discipline that is required of people who dare to
cry: "Spirit of Truth, Set us Free!"

Sub-theme 3: *Spirit of Unity — Reconcile your People!*

The Spirit who sets us free also reconciles us to God in Christ and unites
us into a community of God's people. The Spirit who dwells within us
enables us to appropriate the reconciliation God has offered us in Christ
and to pursue the "ministry of reconciliation entrusted to us".

This common participation in the communion, the koinonia, of the Spirit
helps us to maintain "the unity of the Spirit in the bond of peace". The
gifts of the Spirit build us up together in unity into the "one body", a
"spiritual house" where there is "neither Jew nor Greek... neither slave
nor free... neither male nor female...".

The unity and reconciliation that God intends is for the whole creation, as
witnessed to by God's covenant with Noah and every living creature. The
whole created order is the subject of God's reconciliation.

Through this sub-theme the assembly will seek to clarify further the
nature of the unity we seek — in our search to make manifest the unity
that we have in Christ, in our attempt to articulate and to draw out the

implications of the experience of communion that is ours in the Spirit, though yet to be fully realized, and our understanding of the ecumenical movement as a movement of the Spirit. It will try to understand the full implications of being an inclusive ecclesial communion. It will also attempt to discern the nature of the wider community we seek with people of other faiths and convictions in our search for a world reconciled to God. It will explore the significance of witness, service and sharing in secularized and pluralistic societies.

Sub-theme 4: *Holy Spirit — Transform and Sanctify Us!*

We confess the "Holy" Spirit, for the Spirit is no other than God, close to us and to all creation, with us and in us. The church has confessed the Holy Spirit as the One who brings new life to believers through their regeneration at baptism. In the power of the Spirit every eucharist becomes a celebration of Easter.

At Pentecost, the Spirit transformed the apostolic community into a caring and sharing community rooted in the breaking of bread. The sanctification of lives wrought through the transformation of minds enables believers to bear the fruits of the Spirit.

The Holy Spirit opens up new visions of community, breaking down cultural barriers. The transformation wrought by the Spirit impels us to overcome divisions and confirms us in the search for the renewal of the whole human community. It strengthens and enables us in our struggles against the powers that dehumanize life. Those who are led by the Spirit are God's children and are called to live transformed lives that do not conform to the values of this world.

The Spirit moves in the lives of the saints enabling them to live a life of total self-giving; the Spirit inspires the prophets to call for a transformation of the social order; the Spirit shines through the witness of martyrs who set their hope in God's purposes for the world.

Under this sub-theme the assembly will seek to examine the search for personal renewal and the quest for transformation that underlies the spiritual renewal movements of our day. It will consider the search for liturgical renewal, experiments in new forms of spirituality and church life, and the spirituality rooted in the theologies and modes of community-living that emerge in different parts of the world. It will also explore the spirituality that empowers us in our struggles for justice and peace.

The Bible Studies

Bible study is a learning process. The learning takes place under the guidance of the Holy Spirit. We try to hear what God is telling us through the scriptures. We listen. Such listening, however, involves prayerful preparation.

The biblical books were addressed to situations very different from the ones we are in today. Part of our preparation is to gain some understanding of those situations.

Behind the biblical testimonies lies the twofold conviction that God has a purpose for human history and for all of creation, and within that purpose the people of God have a role. As Christians we share that conviction. But in order to play our role, we must know something of the stage on which it is to be played. That is, we must have an understanding of our own situations. Another part of our preparation, therefore, is to become better informed about our situation.

We want the Bible to "speak" to us. There are indeed biblical texts which seem to "speak" to us directly. But that is not always the case. Often we must consult commentaries and compare notes with others. Any serious Bible study is of necessity a participatory process.

Each of the six studies in this series is based on three passages, one from the Old Testament, one from the Gospels and one from other parts of the New Testament. One of them forms the main text. In the English version of the Bible studies the main texts, reproduced in full here, and quotations from the other texts are all taken from the Revised Standard Version. Wherever we have more than one translation in our language, it will be helpful to compare the way they have rendered the texts we are studying. It is important that we have our Bibles with us as we study the Bible together.

The texts are followed by a short exposition which in turn is followed by a number of comments and testimonies from friends in many parts of the world. These were written specifically to help us in our study of the texts. Living as they do in a variety of situations, these friends look at the biblical passages from very different perspectives. Their insights will enrich our discussions, and their questions will challenge us. We should all be grateful to them; their presence with us as we study the Bible is an authentic ecumenical witness.

Neither the expositions nor the comments of these friends exhaust the meaning of the passages we are studying. All of us must have our own contributions to make and our own way of relating the Word to which we are listening to the world in which we are living. Such contributions may be traditional or radical, conforming or questioning; together they form the ecumenical mosaic of biblical understanding. It should also be possible to share our insights with others, by asking our delegates to make them part of their input in Canberra or by sending them directly to the Bible Studies desk of the WCC.

There are questions we must answer for ourselves. For example, could our groups have an ecumenical composition? Should we invite friends of other faiths to our meetings? What should be the responsibilities of the leader or animator of the group? How many sessions should we plan for each study? How do we prepare for each study? Answers to such questions will depend on our local situation.

It is important that we do not let ourselves be tied down by what is presented in this booklet. We must feel free to make our own comments and tell our own stories. The suggested questions may not be the most relevant questions for us. In that case let us ask our own questions and discuss them instead. We may want to pray in our own words, or make use of prayers from other sources. Let us be as flexible as possible, and as innovative as we can be.

* * *

We are grateful to all the friends who shared with us their comments and testimonies. We regret we have not been able to include all the contributions, but we have made use of their insights in the expositions.

BIBLE STUDY 1

"We believe in the Holy Spirit"

Blessed Lord, you speak to us through the holy scriptures. Grant that we may hear, read, respect, learn and make them our own in such a way that the enduring benefit and comfort of the Word will help us grasp and hold the blessed hope of everlasting life, given us through the Holy Spirit. Amen.

1 Kings 19:9b-18
Luke 24:36-49

Acts 2:1-24, 42-47

from which Judas turned aside, to go to his own place." 26And they cast lots for them, and the lot fell on Matthi'as; and he was enrolled with the eleven apostles.

2 When the day of Pentecost had come, they were all together in one place. 2And suddenly a sound came from heaven like the rush of a mighty wind, and it filled all the house where they were sitting. 3And there appeared to them tongues as of fire, distributed and resting on each one of them. 4And they were all filled with the Holy Spirit and began to speak in other tongues, as the Spirit gave them utterance.

5 Now there were dwelling in Jerusalem Jews, devout men from every nation under heaven. 6And at this sound the multitude came together, and they were bewildered, because each one heard them speaking in his own language. 7And they were amazed and wondered, saying, "Are not all these who are speaking Galileans? 8And how is it that we hear, each of us in his own native language? 9 Par'thians and Medes and E'lamites and residents of Mesopota'mia, Judea and Cappado'cia, Pontus and Asia, 10 Phryg'ia and Pamphyl'ia, Egypt and the parts of Libya belonging to Cyre'ne, and visitors from Rome, both Jews and proselytes, 11 Cretans and Arabians, we hear them telling in our own tongues the mighty works of God." 12And all were amazed and perplexed, saying to one another, "What does this mean?" 13 But others mocking said, "They are filled with new wine."

14 But Peter, standing with the eleven, lifted up his voice and addressed them, "Men of Judea and all who dwell in Jerusalem, let this be known to you, and give ear to my words. 15 For these men are not drunk, as you suppose, since it is only the third hour of the day; 16 but this is what was spoken by the prophet Joel:

17 'And in the last days it shall be, God declares,
    that I will pour out my Spirit upon all flesh,

and your sons and your daughters
    shall prophesy,
and your young men shall see visions,
and your old men shall dream dreams;
18 yea, and on my menservants and my
    maidservants in those days
I will pour out my Spirit; and they
    shall prophesy.
19 And I will show wonders in the heaven
    above
and signs on the earth beneath,
blood, and fire, and vapour of smoke—
20 the sun shall be turned into darkness
and the moon into blood,
before the day of the Lord comes,
    the great and manifest day.
21 And it shall be that whoever calls on
    the name of the Lord shall be
    saved.'
22 "Men of Israel, hear these words:
Jesus of Nazareth, a man attested to you
by God with mighty works and wonders
and signs which God did through him in
your midst, as you yourselves know—
23 this Jesus, delivered up according to
the definite plan and foreknowledge of
God, you crucified and killed by the
hands of lawless men. 24 But God raised
him up, having loosed the pangs of
death, because it was not possible for
him to be held by it. 25 For David says
concerning him,
'I saw the Lord always before me,
for he is at my right hand that I may
    not be shaken;

26 therefore my heart was glad, and my
    tongue rejoiced;
moreover my flesh will dwell in hope.

him." 40And he testified with many
other words and exhorted them, saying,
"Save yourselves from this crooked
generation." 41 So those who received
his word were baptized, and there were
added that day about three thousand
souls. 42And they devoted themselves to
the apostles' teaching and fellowship, to
the breaking of bread and the prayers.
43 And fear came upon every soul;
and many wonders and signs were done
through the apostles. 44And all who believed were together and had all things in
common; 45 and they sold their possessions and goods and distributed them to
all, as any had need. 46And day by day,
attending the temple together and breaking bread in their homes, they partook
of food with glad and generous hearts,
47 praising God and having favour with
all the people. And the Lord added to
their number day by day those who were
being saved.
3 Now Peter and John were going up
to the temple at the hour of prayer,
the ninth hour. 2And a man lame from
birth was being carried, whom they laid

"We believe in the Holy Spirit, the Lord, the giver of
life..." So Christians confess their faith in the words of the
Nicene Creed. But what is the basis of this faith?

Biblical writings tell us of the work of God's Spirit. In the
beginning, when "the earth was without form and void",
the Spirit of God "was moving over the face of the
waters" (Gen. 1:2). The Spirit inspired men and women
to discern and obey the will of God, and to proclaim it
with courage, and bestowed upon them gifts of wisdom,
judgment, leadership and strength. And the same Spirit
empowered Jesus for his earthly ministry.

In the Old Testament the Spirit represents God's univer-
sal presence. It is both a present reality and a promise for

the future when God will pour out the Spirit on all flesh (**Joel 2:28-32;** cf. **Ezek. 37**). In the passage we have chosen from St Luke there is a similar promise. Jesus asks his disciples to stay in the city until they are "clothed with power from on high" (cf. **Acts 1:8, John 14:15-17**).

That promised empowering, the coming of the Comforter, takes place on the day of Pentecost, which is the Feast of First-fruits, and also the festival commemorating the giving of the law on Mount Sinai. We believe as Christians that law and prophecy found their fulfilment in Jesus, and that the promise of Jesus was fulfilled on the day of Pentecost.

The account in **Acts 2,** which we have chosen for our first study, may be divided into three parts. First we have the Pentecost event **(1-13)**. It comprises the coming of the Spirit, the description of which draws on accounts of theophany, the manifestation of God, in the Old Testament, and its effect on the disciples. Filled with the Spirit they speak in other tongues. Whatever else this signifies, it means that they now have the courage to speak, and what they speak is understood by people. In this sense Pentecost restores communication, and the curse of Babel **(Gen. 11:1-9)** is lifted.

In the second part **(14-41)** we have Peter's Pentecost sermon and its impact on people. Inspired by the Spirit, Peter witnesses boldly "that God has made him both Lord and Christ, this Jesus whom you crucified" **(v.36)**.

In the third part **(42-47)** we are given, in a few suggestive verses, a vivid description of the life of the Spirit-filled community. The Spirit comes to an expectant and praying community, and transforms its values and attitudes. The picture is that of a community characterized by its faith in God and its commitment to one another. These too are the gifts of the Spirit.

Pentecost gathered the disciples into the fellowship of the church. It restored communication and understanding. It renewed a people who were living in fear and uncertainty, and strengthened them for mission. It reconfirmed them in their faith, and gave them a new sense of community. And it radically changed their life-style.

The coming of the Spirit was a spectacular event. But should we always associate the Spirit with the unusual and the extraordinary? In the passage from **1 Kings 19** also we have a mighty wind, an earthquake and a fire. When God converses with Elijah, however, it is in "a still small voice" — "the sound of a gentle breeze", according to another translation. What God wants of Elijah is strong action **(15-17)**, but the commission is laid on him in a gentle whisper.

The Spirit often speaks to us in silence, in the quiet of our ordinary life. Signs and wonders are not necessarily the norm. The Spirit is present with us as we live our lives from day to day, and not only in times of crises and in the events that seem to make history.

What does all this mean for us? Before we discuss that, let us listen to the following comments from friends who have been reflecting on the same passages.

Opening up new frontiers

The breath of God comes and dwells in the things we habitually do and makes them new starting points. The traditional feast of Pentecost suddenly gives birth to the young church. The walls give way and the Word travels around and opens up frontiers both for those who receive it and for those who utter it.

The Spirit gathers together, but it also throws things into confusion. It is an event which does not force its meaning upon us; it exposes itself to the hazards of interpretation. It can be cheapened, or it can be read as a sign from God (a few loafers are drunk — or scripture is fulfilled, Acts 2:15-17). And if I choose to recognize the presence of God in history, I am brought to the heart of it, to the cross. In the immediate relevance of preaching, breaking loose from the past, it invites me to look at myself there — as responsible but not left on my own, guilty but freed ("You delivered up Jesus and got rid of him, but according to God's plan; and God raised him up again" 2:23-25).

So then, the ideal community leads me onwards. If I escape the temptation to withdraw into dreams about the beginnings, I find it is like the horizon on my journey, challenging me and keeping me from stopping in my tracks at what discourages or satisfies me. The difficult balance between "all... together" and "to all, as any had need" (2:44f.) has to be achieved afresh and more effectively. The more so because the Spirit does not stop short at the doors of the spiritual, but also overturns the economic order and tests on every level my ability to receive and to give.

Corina Combet-Galland, France

The Spirit should not be quenched

When I meditate on this biblical passage I remember a similar event which occurred in my own country in the fifteenth century. In the turmoils of the Hussite Revolution, amidst all the difficulties, struggles and sufferings, in some places something surfaced which did not exist before: a new fellowship of people. Some towns — more precisely town fortresses — became the centres of a life liberated by the gospel. The population lived in community, with equal rights and duties. It was a community of shared anxieties and hopes. Welcome were all who sought refuge in those towns, landless and poor people as well as those who were relatively rich.

I recall one scene of the film depicting that historical epoch in Czech lands. In the square of the biblically named town Tabor (Joshua 19:12) women and men come forward and with one decisive gesture they throw their money, jewels and other possessions into big containers. They do it under the pressure of the Word of God which they have heard in a new way. They have decided to comply with the challenge of the gospel. They want to follow the life-style of the disciples of Jesus.

Surely the Holy Spirit is not less effective today than in the apostolic or Hussite times. And the Spirit should not be quenched (1 Thess. 5:19). If we open ourselves for the Spirit our creative powers will be mobilized to solve even the most difficult global problems of our times: the issue of hunger in the world and the creation of conditions to ensure the future of life on this planet Earth for us and for coming generations. There is no task which would be more pressing than working for the survival of human kind and the harmony and wholeness of creation.

Jana Opočenská, Czechoslovakia

A miracle of reconciliation

Political developments in my country have unfortunately been along racial lines. In the late 1960s I worked in a district where social relationships between people were

deeply polarized. Communication was impossible. The leaders of the Christian churches and of the Hindu and Muslim communities were concerned. But, beyond that concern, nobody knew what to do.

Finally, some of us decided to meet together, to reflect on what was happening to our district from a faith perspective and to pray for peace. Then we identified and invited party and group leaders to join our meeting for prayer and reflection.

The miracle happened. Not suddenly or dramatically, but gradually and effectively. Hostility died. Communication and social intercourse came to characterize our relationship despite differences in political ideology.

Our vision of a new communal life which transcended those barriers that had hitherto divided us was realized.

That more than anything else has strengthened my belief in the power of the Holy Spirit.

Dale Bisnauth, Guyana

The lesson Elijah learns

My comment is based on the vision Elijah had in **1 Kings 19.** Queen Jezebel threatens to kill him, and the prophet takes refuge in a cave on Mount Horeb. He feels alone and bitter. The people of Israel have forgotten the covenant. Idolatry seems to have triumphed. There is no glimmer of light.

It is in this mood of utter gloom that Elijah has his vision. The servant God, he now learns, is not revengeful but kind and gentle. The storm, the earthquake and the fire do not reveal the divine presence. God speaks, instead, in the whisper of a breeze. The prophet is taught that God's will is not expressed through acts of revenge and violence. What God seeks is the spiritual re-modelling of those who fight for their faith.

Damianos Doikos, Greece

The dawn of a new age

What happened on the day of Pentecost can be understood only in the light of Old Testament prophecies. To a people living without hopes and dreams the prophets brought the promise of a new covenant and a renewed community. They spoke of a time when the law will not be external but written in the heart (Jer.31:33), the dry bones will live (Ezek. 37:10), and dreams and visions abound (Joel 2:28). They pointed to the age of the Spirit.

Pentecost marked the dawn of that age. The prophecy and the fulfilment speak in a very special way to people like us in Latin America, longing for life in its fullness. We know we have a future because of the Spirit. We are convinced that all believers received the gift of the Spirit then, and not just the twelve disciples. We rejoice in the signs of the Spirit among us, the new communities that are coming up and the new impulses that move them. We feel the breath of the Spirit upon our dry bones and we wait in prayer for rebirth and renewal.

Juan Sepúlveda, Chile

Enabling and correcting

Our most concrete relationship with the Holy Spirit is Jesus Christ himself. He promised to send the Spirit to his followers. To be sure, there is a mystical dimension to the Pentecost experience. But it is closely related to life and history, because the same Spirit who empowered Jesus to identify with the broken victims of the injustices of society now descends on his disciples. The Holy Spirit enables us to pursue the ministry of liberation and reconciliation, and at the same time saves us from the moralism which political activism and revolutionary passion so often generate.

The Pentecost experience does not take us out of the struggles of the world; it provides us with a spirituality that equips us for those struggles.

Levi Oracion, Philippines

Questions for discussion

1. What are the Pentecost stories in the life of your church?

2. What are the implications of the affirmation of the Holy Spirit as the Giver of life for our daily life and in our search for community and justice as peoples and nations?

3. Christians are often taken to task for meddling in politics, economics, etc. They are asked to stick to matters spiritual. What is the kind of spirituality that the Spirit requires of us for our times?

Almighty God,
who on the day of Pentecost
sent your Holy Spirit to the disciples
with the wind from heaven and in tongues of flame,
filling them with joy
  and boldness to preach the gospel:
send us out in the power of the same Spirit
to witness to your truth
and to draw all people to the fire of your love;
through Jesus Christ our Lord. Amen.

NOTES

BIBLE STUDY 2

Come, Holy Spirit — Renew
the Whole Creation

O God the Holy Spirit,
come to us, and among us:
   come as the wind, and cleanse us;
   come as the fire, and burn;
   come as the dew, and refresh:
convict, convert, and consecrate
   many hearts and lives
      to our great good
   and thy greater glory,
and this we ask for Jesus Christ's sake. Amen.

Isaiah 65:17-25
Revelation 21:1-5

Luke 1:46-55

"Blessed are you among women, and blessed is the fruit of your womb! 43And why is this granted me, that the mother of my Lord should come to me? 44 For behold, when the voice of your greeting came to my ears, the babe in my womb leaped for joy. 45And blessed is she who believed that there would be^e a fulfilment of what was spoken to her from the Lord."
46 And Mary said,
   "My soul magnifies the Lord,
47 and my spirit rejoices in God my
      Saviour,
48 for he has regarded the low estate of
      his handmaiden.
   For behold, henceforth all generations
      will call me blessed;
49 for he who is mighty has done great
      things for me,
   and holy is his name.
50 And his mercy is on those who fear
      him
   from generation to generation.
51 He has shown strength with his arm,
   he has scattered the proud in the
      imagination of their hearts,
52 he has put down the mighty from their
      thrones,
   and exalted those of low degree;
53 he has filled the hungry with good
      things,
   and the rich he has sent empty away.
54 He has helped his servant Israel,
   in remembrance of his mercy,
55 as he spoke to our fathers,
   to Abraham and to his posterity for
      ever."
56 And Mary remained with her about three months, and returned to her home.

In our first study we sought to make our own the confession of the church through the centuries. Joining the company of believers at all times and in all places, we confess that we believe in the Holy Spirit. That confession has its origin in the outpouring of the Spirit on the day of Pentecost. We saw how that event inspired and revitalized a small band of people, and inaugurated the Christian movement.

But the coming of the Spirit was not a closed, once-for-all happening. Even as we thank God for the gift of the Spirit to the early Christians, and rejoice in the Spirit's presence with us and with all believers, we pray that we too may be inspired and renewed. Not only we, but all of God's creation.

The passage from **Isaiah 65** is in line with the renewing work of the Spirit. Its theme is the total and comprehensive restoration of God's world.

Recall the refrain in the creation story in **Genesis 1**: "And God saw it was good." That is no longer the case. Now the whole world stands in need of renewal — men and women, systems and structures, things animate and inanimate, all of nature.

The prophet's message of hope is addressed to a people who have emerged out of the harrowing experience of exile, and it promises an end to suffering and oppression. God will once again rejoice in creation and restore communication with people; in fact God will answer even before they call, and hear "while they are yet speaking". The work of their hands will be blessed (cf. **Psalm 90:17**) and their labour will not be in vain. People will not exploit people: "they shall not plant and another eat". The reconciliation that is promised is total — with God, with nature and between people.

The renewal that is projected in the passage from **Revelation 21** transcends time and space. It is an eschatological vision, a vision of the last things. "Then I saw a new heaven and a new earth", writes the author of the book, and the sea, in biblical writings often the symbol of chaos and alienation, "was no more".

But it is *God* who makes all things new. God *makes* them new; renewal is a continuing process, not like a book that one reads and, having read, puts aside. What God makes new are *all things,* not just us and our churches. And God renews us and all things by dwelling with us, wiping away every tear from our eyes and involving us too in the work of renewal.

But how shall this be?, we ask, as Mary did. "The Holy Spirit will come upon you", the angel said to Mary, "and the power of the Most High will overshadow you" **(Luke 1:35)**. Mary accepted God's plan for her, and consciously received the Spirit. She was not a passive woman acquiescing in a decision made for her; she decided, fully aware of what the social consequences would be, to play her part in the coming of the Son of God into the world to save the world. That was why she could make her own this great song of praise and adoration, of total dedication and unquenchable hope.

The Magnificat is not an original song. Another woman, Hannah, the mother of Samuel, had prayed in much the same words **(1 Sam. 2:1-10)**. But what is original is the context, and the commitment. The song begins with what God has done for her, an ordinary village woman. That, for her, is the symbol and guarantee of the renewal and transformation of all areas of life, reversing roles and changing structures.

No wonder the Magnificat has provided inspiration and strength for Christians in every generation. In our own times it is widely used by men and women who struggle against political oppression, economic exploitation and social and racial discrimination. They believe in the power of the Spirit, as Mary did.

30

A Prayer

Where families are fractured
by domestic upheavals
and children forced on to streets
to fight for survival,

Where more resources are spent
on arms and destruction
and less attention paid
to sickness and starvation,

Come Holy Spirit
Heal our wounds
Renew the Whole Creation!

Where the acquisition of things
has become an obsession
and the worth of a human being
is measured by one's possessions,

Where our air, trees and seas
are besieged by pollution
and purblind mercenary greed
threatens our environment,

Come Holy Spirit
Heal our wounds
Renew our Whole Creation!

Where countries are split apart
by communalism and racism
and innocent blood is spilt
by wanton acts of terrorism,

Where internecine warfare
sets nation against nation
and a nuclear holocaust
looms ominous on our horizon,

Come Holy Spirit
Heal our wounds
Renew the Whole Creation!

Cecil Rajendra, Malaysia

Turning surprise into joy

Mary goes to see her elderly relative, Elizabeth, "the barren one" as they perhaps called her with a certain contempt.

The two women meet, and, for the first time in Luke's Gospel, the Holy Spirit *is* present. Up to now we have had two references to the Spirit's presence in future terms: Zechariah's son "*will* be filled with the Holy Spirit" from his birth. "The Holy Spirit *will* come on you" is the assurance given to Mary herself. But when Mary went into Zechariah's house, Elizabeth "*was* filled with the Holy Spirit".

As we accompany Mary on her journey from Nazareth to the hills of Judea, we tend to imagine a woman who is surprised and troubled by the angel's message, by the fact of her own pregnancy. But only until she reaches her cousin's home. Then Mary's troubled surprise is transformed into joy, a joy which erupts into song.

It is one of the old songs of her people. Both women will have known it all their lives. But suddenly it has come alive... in the presence of the Spirit and the certainty that God does "great things". God, using their willingness, creates and re-creates the kingdom in this world, because the Spirit at work in them allows them to say: "Let your will be done in me."

At Christmas time the children of our Sunday schools dramatize these scenes of the gospel: the annunciation, the visitation, the stable and the manger, the shepherds, angels and magi. For brief moments the children become the main actors, perspiring under long robes in the heat of the Christmas season in the southern hemisphere. They lend their voices and gestures to the women and men Luke presents to us with such sobriety. They become the actors of a story whose main protagonist is the Holy Spirit — the Spirit who, on the stage of this world, transforms our surprise into joy whenever we can discern what God is doing in us.

Carlos Delmonte, Uruguay

But when, O Lord, and how?

On 1 March 1986, I was released from prison by the new government under President Aquino. Like most political prisoners, I was happy to be outside the bars. But I could not help worrying about the freedom of the many, not just from dictatorship, but also from poverty and injustice.

To express my mixed feelings, I grasped for an image. "I feel as if I were witnessing the birth of a premature baby. It came sooner than expected. It's smaller than what we wanted. But it is a baby — we should be happy. At the same time, we should worry — will it live?"

Somehow, without consciously straining after it, the Song of Mary offered some insights. "He has put down the mighty from their throne and has exalted the lonely. He has filled the hungry with good things, and has sent the rich away, empty." Yes, a mighty dictator had been put down. But will the lowly be uplifted? Or will the one mighty be replaced by a committee of mighty?

Some of our very rich have been sent away, but not empty. They took along a lot, to add on to the lot they had sent out of the Philippines years before. And many more have not even found the need to go away. They switched sides and stay on.

Blessed are those who hunger and thirst after justice. But when, O Lord, and how?

Ed de la Torre, Philippines

Mary's Song down under

Australians squirm if you ask them to talk about God. Politics, yes. Sport, by all means. But not religion. God-talk, they suspect, is empty speculation. It creates discord. Its abstractions don't connect with the urgent issues of life. There is no faster way to wreck a good party on Bondi Beach than by dragging divinity into it.

But Mary's words are not about the God of casual conversation. Here is not the bored musing of the sun-drenched crowd.

Mary's God is a verb, not an abstract noun. This God acts, shocks, surprises, turns the world upside down, shatters humanity's facile expectations, cuts through our religiosity too.

This God is not to be speculated about over a can of beer on a Sydney beach. But to be praised, with gratitude and amazed joy.

David Gill, Australia

The inevitable liberation

Mary's song of joy is an indictment of the South African regime. We in this country who are part of the oppressed masses are assured by her words that liberation is inevitable. We are assured that God cares for us. We know from history that God scatters the proud.

We know from the struggles that are waged daily by our people that rulers will be brought down from their thrones and the "people *shall* truly govern" in the spirit of the Freedom Charter. God has seen the plight of the workers and the peasantry in our community. God has seen how people are dehumanized and exploited. God will give power to the powerless in our community. That process has begun already. The brutality of the regime is testimony to that. People have realized that liberation is coming no matter what. They are therefore engaged in student organizations, in trade unions, in civic organizations, in relevant church structures, to galvanize this massive force for a free and just South Africa.

The Magnificat is a message of hope for the people in South Africa. It says to us that the God of history is still alive. God is in charge. Our victory is God's victory.

Bafana Khumalo, South Africa

Called to be God-bearer

As an African woman (a nun) this text speaks to me in a special way for, like Mary, God has done great things for me; he has called me out of nothingness to life, love, health and vocation. Like Mary, an unknown African woman is lifted up, called to be a God-bearer, to dedicate my entire self to the service of the creator of the universe... Praying the Magnificat leads me into contemplative participation. The distinctive parallelism and rhythm of the song produce a repetitive pattern, a going back and forth that deepens my experience. It involves me fully in the experience of hearing; it calls for a response not only of my mind, but of my feelings and my body as well. My whole person is invited to enter into its meaning. It invites me to step into the text with my whole self, just as the rhythm of music invites me to join the dance.... Like Mary, I become God-bearer to the poor, the oppressed — with the words of life.

Rosemary Edet, Nigeria

Mary represents us here

Mary represents us here. The Central American woman lives in poverty and servitude. We have been subdued, and marginalized from the structures of society. Here we see a woman, in many ways like us, who is favoured by God and chosen to transform humanity. Thus the example of Mary enables us to challenge traditional roles which society assigned to us and to begin a struggle to transform the present reality plagued with injustice and war.

We feel strengthened, and we dare to confront the powerful and mighty, and to ask them to give back our sons and daughters, our husbands and friends who have been forcefully taken away. We are inspired to change this world into one in which there are no more forceful disappearances and cruel torture, and our basic rights are respected, in which there is no discrimination because of the colour of our skins, our ethnic ancestry, or because of our gender, age or lack of purchasing power. We take courage from Mary, and we wait upon the Spirit.

Raquel Rodriguez, Costa Rica

A turning point in her life

Maria was a drug addict. After she was cured, she took part in a television round-table discussion on the growing drug problem. The programme presented statistical data, sociological explanations, police reports, legal perspectives, etc. Among all the learned presentations Maria's simple testimony stood out.

Maria said: "When I was first involved in drugs, my life had no meaning. My family gave me whatever I asked for. I was at the centre, and the world revolved round me. Indeed I was a poor, empty girl. I had no time for a flower or a bird; I had no concern for the poor or the victims of injustice. When I was undergoing treatment at a foundation, I longed to get back to the cocaine friends. Then, walking in the park one August evening, I heard the Magnificat being sung at the foundation chapel. That was the turning point of my life. Our Lady Theotokos spoke to me through her song. She invited me to commit myself to her son, our Lord, and find meaning and love in my life."

During the first 13 days of August, every evening there is a special service for Theotokos in our churches. Maria must have heard the Magnificat sung at one of these services. The experts on narcomania listened to her testimony with a certain ironic sympathy.

Dimitra Koukoura, Greece

Questions for discussion

We have listened to the different ways the song of Mary has spoken to Christians in different parts of the world. We should perhaps begin by sharing with each other aspects of the text that speak most meaningfully to us. The following questions may help us to continue our discussion of the passage.

1. A Nigerian Christian writes that "Mary is the prototype of the renewed people of God; only the redeemed can sing like her". Do you agree? Why, in your opinion, was Mary chosen by God? Who are the "God-bearers" today?

2. An Argentinian comment on this text says that it is a challenge to "those who think that the world of the Spirit does not intersect with the worlds of the market place, the battle-field, or the political arena ... It reminds me of the strange fact that at the height of the so-called 'dirty-war' in Argentina, while the military junta was engaged in clandestine acts of violence against the civilian populace, those same rulers declared that it was henceforth a crime against the state to read or sing the Magnificat."

   What are the social and political implications of believing in the renewing work of the Spirit for your own community and nation?

3. What is your vision of a renewed church, a renewed community? What can be done to activate your vision? What role do you envisage for yourself in that process?

O God, life-giving Spirit,
Spirit of healing and comfort,
of integrity and truth,
we believe and trust in you.
Warm-winged Spirit, brooding over creation,
rushing wind and Pentecostal fire,
we commit ourselves to work with you
and renew our world. Amen.

NOTES

BIBLE STUDY 3

Giver of Life — Sustain your Creation!

We praise you, Holy Spirit, our Advocate and Comforter.
 Help us to affirm life
  in the midst of death,
 supporting us as we confront the power of destruction,
 urging us to hammer swords into ploughs
  and spears into pruningknives;
 so that wolves and sheep
  live together in peace,
 life is celebrated,
  creation is restored
  as the sphere of the living.
 Holy Spirit, we praise you;
  help us to affirm life
   in the midst of death. Amen.

Romans 8:1-27
John 3:1-8

Genesis 1:1-2:4a

1 In the beginning God created[a] the heavens and the earth. 2 The earth was without form and void, and darkness was upon the face of the deep; and the Spirit[b] of God was moving over the face of the waters.

3 And God said, "Let there be light"; and there was light. 4And God saw that the light was good; and God separated the light from the darkness. 5 God called the light Day, and the darkness he called Night. And there was evening and there was morning, one day.

6 And God said, "Let there be a firmament in the midst of the waters, and let it separate the waters from the waters." 7And God made the firmament and separated the waters which were under the firmament from the waters which were above the firmament. And it was so. 8And God called the firmament Heaven. And there was evening and there was morning, a second day.

9 And God said, "Let the waters under the heavens be gathered together into one place, and let the dry land appear." And it was so. 10 God called the dry land Earth, and the waters that were gathered together he called Seas. And God saw that it was good. 11And God

42

said, "Let the earth put forth vegetation, plants yielding seed, and fruit trees bearing fruit in which is their seed, each according to its kind, upon the earth." And it was so. 12 The earth brought forth vegetation, plants yielding seed according to their own kinds, and trees bearing fruit in which is their seed, each according to its kind. And God saw that it was good. 13And there was evening and there was morning, a third day.

14 And God said, "Let there be lights in the firmament of the heavens to separate the day from the night; and let them be for signs and for seasons and for days and years, 15 and let them be lights in the firmament of the heavens to give light upon the earth." And it was so. 16And God made the two great lights, the greater light to rule the day, and the lesser light to rule the night; he made the stars also. 17And God set them in the firmament of the heavens to give light upon the earth, 18 to rule over the day and over the night, and to separate the light from the darkness. And God saw that it was good. 19And there was evening and there was morning, a fourth day.

20 And God said, "Let the waters bring forth swarms of living creatures, and let birds fly above the earth across the firmament of the heavens." 21 So God created the great sea monsters and every living creature that moves, with which the waters swarm, according to their kinds, and every winged bird according to its kind. And God saw that it was good. 22And God blessed them, saying, "Be fruitful and multiply and fill the waters in the seas, and let birds multiply on the earth." 23And there was evening and there was morning, a fifth day.

24 And God said, "Let the earth bring forth living creatures according to their kinds: cattle and creeping things and beasts of the earth according to their kinds." And it was so. 25And God made the beasts of the earth according to their kinds and the cattle according to their kinds, and everything that creeps upon the ground according to its kind. And God saw that it was good.

26 Then God said, "Let us make man in our image, after our likeness; and let them have dominion over the fish of the sea, and over the birds of the air, and over the cattle, and over all the earth, and over every creeping thing that creeps upon the earth." 27 So God created man in his own image, in the image of God he created him; male and female he created them. 28And God blessed them, and God said to them, "Be fruitful and multiply, and fill the earth and subdue it; and have dominion over the fish of the sea and over the birds of the air and over every living thing that moves upon the earth." 29And God said, "Behold, I have given you every plant yielding seed which is upon the face of all the earth, and every tree with seed in its fruit; you shall have them for food. 30And to every beast of the earth, and to every bird of the air, and to everything that creeps on the earth, everything that has the breath of life, I have given every green plant for food." And it was so. 31And God saw everything that he had made, and behold, it was very good. And there was evening and there was morning, a sixth day.

2 Thus the heavens and the earth were finished, and all the host of them. 2And on the seventh day God finished his work which he had done, and he rested on the seventh day from all his work which he had done. 3 So God blessed the seventh day and hallowed it, because on it God rested from all his work which he had done in creation.

4 These are the generations of the heavens and the earth when they were created.

In the day that the LORD God made the earth and the heavens, 5 when no plant of the field was yet in the earth and no herb of the field had yet sprung up— for the LORD God had not caused it to rain upon the earth, and there was no man to till the ground; 6 but a mist^c went up from the earth and watered the whole face of the ground—7 then the LORD God formed man of dust from the ground, and breathed into his nostrils the breath of life; and man became a living being. 8And the LORD God planted a garden in Eden, in the east; and there he put the man whom he had formed. 9And out of the ground the LORD God made to grow every tree that is pleasant to the sight and good for food, the tree of life also in the midst of the garden, and the tree of the knowledge of good and evil.

10 A river flowed out of Eden to water the garden, and there it divided and became four rivers. 11 The name of the first is Pishon; it is the one which

The Bible begins with two distinct stories of creation (see **2:4b-25**). The first, on which we focus in this study, gives an account of the creation of the universe. The central affirmation it makes is that God created all things, giving form to the formless and bringing order out of chaos.

That means we should not attribute divine powers to anything in the created world. Neither the greater and lesser lights of heaven nor the trees and animals of the earth "according to their kinds" can be considered as divine. Not even the human being created in the image and likeness of God, with whom God has a special relationship and on whom is laid the responsibility to care for and preserve the earth.

"In the beginning, God..." We immediately call to mind the familiar verses with which the author of the Fourth Gospel begins the story of Jesus' life and work: "In the beginning was the Word, and the Word was with God, and the Word was God. He was in the beginning with God; all things were made through him, and without him was not anything made that was made" **(John 1:1-3)**. And a few verses later, the bold statement that the Word "became flesh and dwelt among us, full of grace and truth" **(v.14)**.

In the Genesis passage we are studying, there is a similar statement about the role of the Spirit of God in creation. The heavens and the earth have been created. "Now the earth was a formless void, there was darkness over the deep, and God's Spirit hovered over the water" (JB). Like a bird hovering over her young ones.

In both Hebrew and Greek the word for "spirit" often means "wind" or "breath". In biblical usage spirit can also be the breath of life; when it is withdrawn life is extinguished **(Ps. 146:4;** cf. **Job 33:4)**. Used of God, spirit is the life-giving power. Creation itself, according to the Bible, is the act by which God calls into being all of reality. It is through the Spirit, as it is through Jesus Christ, the Word and Wisdom of God, that creation takes place. And it is by the Spirit that creation — all that is called into being by God — is sustained.

Israel's faith insisted on the historical character of human existence. Yahweh is the Lord of history, and the community understood itself as the people of God. The creation stories in Genesis evolved out of this self-understanding of Israel. They are made up of elements borrowed from the mythologies of local religions, but they are presented as history. They are seen as defining Israel's identity as the people of God. In that self-understanding, the Lord of history is also the God of all creation.

In course of time the doctrine of creation thus became fundamental to Jewish faith. For us as Christians it has always been an article of faith. We confess, in the words of the Nicene Creed: "We believe in one God, the Father almighty, Maker of heaven and earth, and of all things visible and invisible."

There is another approach to creation in the Bible which is doxological rather than historical. In the Book of Job and in several psalms there are passages where the whole creation is involved in singing the praise of God (see, for example, **Psalms 19** and **104**). This Wisdom tradition projects a more harmonious view of creation which can serve as a corrective to the more human-centred historical understanding.

Because Israel thus thought of creation as a historical event, the first among "the mighty acts of God", it is incorporated into the covenant God has made with the people. In that sense it is also the first saving act of God **(Ps. 74:12-17)**. Creation, therefore, has a soteriological or redemptive dimension. And, inasmuch as God's plan of salvation is being worked out through a continuous process of re-creation, redemption has itself a creative dimension.

The New Testament sees the redemptive work of Jesus Christ as "new creation", and the Spirit of God, now clearly identified as the Holy Spirit, is the agent of all re-creation.

Considering the time when John's Gospel was written (probably about 90 A.D.), it is more than likely that the passage we are studying reflects the belief in regeneration or rebirth associated with baptism. Such regeneration happens through the Spirit whose workings are beyond human understanding. Those who are born of water and of the Spirit become part of God's redemptive work in history wrought by the Spirit. They are part of the "new creation"; they are also agents of the "new creation".

In **Romans 8** Paul had already taken much further this idea that the redemption offered in Christ is a creative act of God. Paul applies it to the whole created order. The "new creation" has become a reality in Christ. We are ourselves part of it. But its full realization is in the future; and then it will embrace all things and all people.

The original creative act of God brought all of creation into existence. Human sin, however, alienates us from creation, and threatens to destroy it. Now it is the whole creation that waits with eager longing to be set free by the power of the Spirit. We who are saved by the life and death and resurrection of Christ and have the first fruits of the Spirit must be involved with the Spirit in this ongoing work of re-creation.

The message for us is the same as in the Genesis story of creation. Human beings are given the responsibility for the right ordering and preservation of what God has made. We are appointed stewards of the earth. We must work for the sustaining of the gifts of creation. We are called to a caring partnership with the Spirit in the work of recreating our world.

But how? The following comments and testimonies may help us as we try to answer that question.

Loving each other and the garden

"In order to love each other,
We have to love the garden.
In order to love the garden,
We have to love each other."
(United Church of Canada, 1977)

It was important to watch for the sign as I sped along in my car. It was such a small community that one could easily miss it. From the highway it appeared to be only a gas station and a restaurant, but it was the half-way point of the journey, and a good place to pause. Suddenly I saw the signboard that said, "That was English River", and I hastily put on the brakes and drew over to a parking place. Time for a break and some fresh fish.

I don't stop there any more now. Behind the gas station and the restaurant was an extensive beautiful river system that drained many of the lakes of Northern Ontario in that part of Canada. The rivers and lakes had abundant fish, and it was one of the main popular fishing resorts for American tourists who were guided on their trips by native people. The fish of that river system also sustained the lives of Indian tribes whose reserves bordered the lakes and streams.

A pulp and paper mill upstream poisoned the waterway with chemical waste, and destroyed the sick, disaffected native population with mercury poisoning found in the fish. For the tourists, it was loss of fun. For the native people, it was loss of eyesight, or of limbs, or of life. A commission of inquiry called itself "Northern Frontier, Northern Homeland", because the frontier for humankind *is* to sustain our homeland.

The native people of Canada, before they enter the sweatlodge for purification ceremonies, offer a prayer for "all the relations". That means all their immediate family, all human beings, all animals and non-human substances, every grub or rock, all of creation itself. They are teaching us to become lovers of each other and of the garden. Unless we do, we perish.

Lois Wilson, Canada

A testimony from Brazil

"A terra é de todos, disse Deus a Adâo
Toma e cultiva, tira dela o teu pão."
(The land belongs to all, said God to Adam.
Take it and till it, and receive your bread.)

That was their refrain in the early eighties. The 12 million landless farmers and peasants of Brazil were without form, lacking consciousness and organization. They were migrating for low-paid jobs, passing by large tracts of mostly uncultivated land. But the Spirit of God was moving them. They formed groups, started local organizations and later a strong national movement. The light was separated from the darkness when they realized that the authorities were a tool of the landlords and the ruling class. They decided to occupy the vacant land. They experienced Emmanuel — God with us in community. They worked on the land and the land put forth plants yielding seeds and fruits. What they produced was for their survival, not for export. On a day of pilgrimage in the south, more than 20,000 landless people distributed

seeds of Araucaria trees for reforestation. What the big timber companies had destroyed, the small people would restore.

But thousands of them are still living in camps along the roads, keeping alive the struggle for agrarian reform. But more land will be liberated from exploitation. And God blesses men, women and children, created in the divine image, as they share and work on the earth in a sharing community.

Werner Fuchs, Brazil

From a Hindu context

The creation story of Genesis 1 reminds me of the Hymn of Creation in the tenth book of the Rig Veda, the most ancient of the Hindu scriptures.

The Vedic hymn also speaks of "the beginning" as enveloped in darkness. There was nothing except the undifferentiated (chaotic) waters and the void: "There was not the non-existent nor the existent then; there was not the air nor the heaven which is beyond. There was not death nor immortality then. There was not the beacon of night nor of day (moon nor sun)."

Unlike some other Hindu myths that attribute the creative initiative to God, the Vedic poem ends with a question which is also answered in part: "Who shall here declare whence it has been produced? Who then knows whence this creation has arisen? He who is in the highest heaven is its surveyor, he only knows." There is a refreshing honesty in the Rig-Vedic hymn. God only knows where the universe comes from and how it has been established!

The author of Genesis 1 is faced with the same mystery of a universe whose origin is beyond human comprehension. His thoughts move in yet another direction: "In the beginning," he says, "God created the heavens and the earth." The whole of Jewish faith, life and history, as that of Christians who inherit this confession, depends on this

49

daring affirmation. Take away the belief that God created the world, loves it and is involved in its history, nothing else will make sense in Judaism and Christianity. Everything else in the Bible is founded on this simple confession: "The earth is the Lord's and the fullness thereof; the world and those that dwell therein."

Isn't the crisis of faith in our day ultimately a crisis of faith about creation? Whether it is the ecological crisis, issues of economic justice and peace or the terrifying spectre of a nuclear disaster, in the last analysis these things are about what we believe creation to be — and to whom it belongs. "In the beginning God" and "in the end God" are the two pillars of faith. In between is creation and the unfolding of human life in history — sustained by the power of the Spirit.

S. Jeyaraj, India

The importance of the beginning for now

Our beliefs on "the beginning" have important consequences for our life here and now. In my country, for example, with at least seven prominent ethnic groups, all of them with distinct stories of "the beginning", how do we relate to one another? And how do we relate to the Genesis story?

The story of the Karen people is largely based on a moral approach. The higher spirits made mistakes and were demoted as human beings. Having learned their lesson, human beings now attach a great deal of importance to moral conduct or right relationships in community. For the Burman, following an Indian tradition, Mount Meru is the place where everything began. Because of their connection with Mount Meru, the Burmans too are at the centre, a particular understanding of the beginning which leads to self-affirmation. This has had its effect on Burmese history. The question is, how do we live together and shape a common future? One wishes there were one single creation story, with the Creator and the created!

Sann Sann Myint, Burma

Our islands are God's creation

Each Pacific island nation has its own creation story. Kiribati too has one. The creator is known as Nareau. Is he the creator-God of the Genesis story?

The details differ, but both stories agree that what we see around us is created by Someone (Genesis calls him God, a general term; Kiribati calls him "God" too, but we have a specific name for him).

If we are talking about the same God in these stories, then our islands too have their origin in God. How wonderful to behold the beauty of creation around us! There is harmony and peace here, but alas, darkness too. Our islands are threatened by evil forces, from within and from outside. Modern science and technology cannot help. They too have become agents of darkness without knowing it. And if they know, they are willing to serve human ambition and power.

But who controls our lives and all of nature, and to whom shall we ascribe honour, power and might? It is God who creates and sustains, the Mighty One who creates light out of darkness. The islands are accountable to no one but God alone, who is the Creator and the Hope of all.

Baiteke Nabetari, Kiribati

Corn Mother: an American Indian story

For tribes with horticultural interests, stories recounting the origin of planting take on enormous significance. Most importantly these stories show the link between the land, food, people and the ancestors who are buried in the land. The story of Corn Mother, for instance, is much more than an interesting but fanciful story of a simple people in need of simple explanations of the world. On the contrary, it is a complex story which helps establish the foundation for a consistent cosmological whole. To that extent it is a theological story.

Now the people increased and became numerous. They lived by hunting, and the more people there were, the less game they found. They were hunting it out, and as the

animals decreased, starvation came upon the people. And First Mother pitied them.

The little children came to First Mother and said: "We are hungry. Feed us." But she had nothing to give them, and she wept. She told them: "Be patient. I will make some food. Then your little bellies will be full." But she kept weeping.

Her husband asked: "How can I make you smile? How can I make you happy?"
"There is only one thing that will stop my tears."
"What is it?" asked her husband.
"It is this: you must kill me."
"I could never do that."
"You must, or I will go on weeping and grieving forever."

Then the husband travelled far, to the end of the earth, to the north he went, to ask the Great Instructor, his uncle Kloskurbeh, what he should do.

"You must do what she wants. You must kill her," said Kloskurbeh. Then the young man went back to his home, and it was his turn to weep. But First Mother said: "Tomorrow at high noon you must do it. After you have killed me, let two of our sons take hold of my hair and drag my body over that empty patch of earth. Let them drag me back and forth, back and forth, over every part of the patch, until all my flesh has been torn from my body. Afterwards, take my bones, gather them up, and bury them in the middle of this clearing. Then leave that place."

She smiled and said: "Wait seven moons and then come back, and you will find my flesh there, flesh given out of love, and it will nourish and strengthen you for ever and ever."

So it was done. The husband slew his wife, and her sons, praying, dragged her body to and fro as she had commanded, until her flesh covered all the earth. Then they took up her bones and buried them in the middle of it. Weeping loudly, they went away.

When the husband and his children and his children's children came back to that place after seven moons had passed, they found the earth covered with tall, green, tasselled plants. The plants' fruit — corn — was First Mother's flesh, given so that the people might live and flourish. And they partook of First Mother's flesh and found it sweet beyond words. Following her instructions, they did not eat all, but put many kernels back into the earth. In this way her flesh and spirit renewed themselves every seven months, generation after generation.

George E. Tinker, USA

Questions for discussion

1. Most religions have their own creation stories. If you know any, share them with the group. What in your opinion are the special emphases in the biblical account of creation?

2. It is often said that the biblical tradition, which appears to set the human being over, and apart from, creation, is mainly responsible for our present ecological crisis. Do you agree?

3. We affirm that God created all things. What are the implications of that affirmation (a) for the way we relate to one another as individuals, communities and nations, and (b) for the way we relate to the non-human part of creation?

O Great Spirit,
  whose breath gives life to the world,
  and whose voice is heard in the soft breeze:
We need your strength and wisdom.
Cause us to walk in beauty. Give us eyes
  ever to behold the red and purple sunset.
Make us wise so that we may understand
  what you have taught us.
Help us learn the lessons you have hidden
  in every leaf and rock.
Make us always ready to come to you
  with clean hands and steady eyes,
so when life fades, like the fading sunset,
  our spirits may come to you without shame. Amen.

NOTES

BIBLE STUDY 4

Spirit of Truth — Set us Free!

L: The wind of the Spirit challenges us to change:
P: Give us courage to respond, O God.

L: The fire of the Spirit calls us
   to a passion for the kingdom:
P: Warm us and give us your energy, O God.

L: The breath of the Spirit offers us new life:
P: May we receive and live out the Gospel in the world.

L: In a world where there is need and oppression,
   violence and alienation
P: May we bring life and love, O God.

L: In a world where there is racism,
   hatred and division
P: May we bring unity and community, O God.

L: In a world where there is meaninglessness and
   emptiness:
P: May we bring purpose and hope, O God.

L: Lead us forth, Spirit of God,
   in joy and in faith,
   in truth and in freedom:
P: In ways known and unknown, may we follow.

   Amen.

Galatians 5:1-13,25
John 15:26,27; 16:4b-15

Isaiah 61:1-4

---

21 Your people shall all be righteous;
　　they shall possess the land for ever,
　the shoot of my planting, the work
　　of my hands,
　　that I might be glorified.
22 The least one shall become a clan,
　　and the smallest one a mighty
　　nation;
　I am the LORD;
　　in its time I will hasten it.

61 The Spirit of the Lord GOD is
　　upon me,
　because the LORD has anointed
　　me
to bring good tidings to the
　afflicted;[m]
he has sent me to bind up the
　brokenhearted,
to proclaim liberty to the captives,
　and the opening of the prison[n] to
　those who are bound;
2 to proclaim the year of the LORD's
　favour,
　and the day of vengeance of our
　God;
to comfort all who mourn;
3 to grant to those who mourn in
　Zion—

to give them a garland instead of
　ashes,
the oil of gladness instead of
　mourning,
the mantle of praise instead of a
　faint spirit;
that they may be called oaks of
　righteousness,
　the planting of the LORD, that he
　may be glorified.
4 They shall build up the ancient ruins,
　they shall raise up the former
　devastations;
they shall repair the ruined cities,
　the devastations of many
　generations.

5 Aliens shall stand and feed your
　flocks,
　foreigners shall be your ploughmen
　and vinedressers;
6 but you shall be called the priests of
　the LORD,
　men shall speak of you as the
　ministers of our God;
you shall eat the wealth of the
　nations,
　and in their riches you shall
　glory.

The question Pilate asked Jesus, "What is truth?", is better known than the statement that provoked it. "For this I was born", Jesus said to Pilate, "and for this I have come into the world, to bear witness to the truth" **(John 18:37,38)**. To those who believed in him Jesus said: "If you continue in my word, you are truly my disciples, and you will know the truth, and the truth will make you free" **(John 8:31,32)**.

Perhaps Pilate was cynical, and his question only rhetorical. But it cannot be dismissed as irrelevant. It is a fundamental question, and philosophers and scientists have been trying to answer it for centuries. Without much success.

For us as Christians the answer to that question is simple, though its implications are not. To know the truth, for us, is to abide in Jesus' love even as he abides in his Father's love, and to love one another as he loves us (**John 15:10-12**). Only the Spirit of God can guide us into such experience of truth to which the church and tradition bear witness.

In the passage from St John we read that the Spirit of truth will reveal to us the truth about God, about Jesus himself, and about the world.

The Spirit will "convince the world concerning sin, righteousness and judgment" (**16:8**). As Counsellor or Advocate the Spirit will argue, expose and judge, enabling us to identify the forces that keep us in bondage.

Paul's letter to the Galatian Christians is a passionate defence of the freedom that we have in Jesus Christ. In the passage we are studying, Paul dwells on the paradox that authentic freedom is to be found only in loving service. His thesis is that the Spirit sets us free to serve.

Paul is acutely conscious of the powers that enslave people (see **Gal. 4:3; Eph. 6:12**). Galatian Christians are now tempted to move away from the faith that had set them free. They would rather rely on their own works than on their faith in the crucified and risen Lord. The Spirit had led them into the truth, and that truth had set them free; now, insists Paul, if we live by the Spirit, we should also walk by the Spirit.

The freedom into which the Holy Spirit leads us is both personal and social. We are renewed as individuals so that, bearing the fruits of the Spirit, we can be recreated as communities and nations. Paul exhorts the Galatian Christians not to give in to the desires of human nature, but stand fast in the freedom in Christ, to be obedient to the truth and to walk by the Spirit — all these made possible by the power of the Spirit.

The passage to which we turn now — and on which we focus in this study — is of special importance to Christian people everywhere. Jesus began his earthly ministry by reading in public the first verses of **Isaiah 61.** Let us recall the context.

After his baptism, when he was praying, "the Holy Spirit descended upon him in bodily form, as a dove" **(Luke 3:22)**. He returned from Jordan "full of the Holy Spirit", and was "led by the Spirit for forty days in the wilderness, tempted by the devil" **(4:1,2)**. "In the power of the Spirit" he goes back to Galilee. On the sabbath, at the synagogue in Nazareth, he reads these verses — and then announces: "Today this scripture has been fulfilled in your hearing" **(4:18-21)**.

That is a clear indication of what Jesus understood his ministry to be. No wonder the passage is often referred to as the Nazareth manifesto. It relates to the old prophetic message of the good tidings of the new era pressing in, of the time when God's will will be done on earth. That time, early Christians like Luke were convinced, is *now*.

The last eleven chapters of Isaiah were probably written after the difficult and soul-searching period of the Babylonian exile. The exiles are back in their own country now, but their situation has not improved. In some respects it has deteriorated. The poor are becoming poorer, and their number is increasing. Injustice is rampant. The freedom they longed for has not been realized. They have only exchanged an external slavery for a more insidious internal bondage. There is no sign of the expected Messiah. The Holy City is still in ruins. There is mounting frustration and, among the well-to-do, growing secularization.

That is the social context in which the writer of this chapter presents a daring prophetic profile of "the year of the Lord's favour". Addressing a context marked by a crisis of faith and a crisis of hope, the prophet, inspired by the Spirit of God, announces a message of total liberation which will be achieved through a process of releasing and restoring.

Setting people free is a basic biblical theme. The Exodus and the return from exile in Babylon were landmarks in Israelite history, and they have become paradigms of deliverance. In the New Testament Jesus is seen as the one who delivers us from the bondage of sin and suffer-ing. He is the Christ, the Anointed of the Spirit; he is also the "servant" of God whose ears are open to God and who identifies with his people. He both judges and saves. He proclaims "the year of the Lord's favour and the day of vengeance of our God" — the *year* because God is patient, the *day* because God is just.

The *year* recalls the Jubilee Year of **Leviticus 25,** every fiftieth year when the land should be restored to those who originally possessed it. Under its operation slaves would be freed and all debts discharged. It is a measure that prevents permanent disinheritance, lasting depend-ence and perpetual poverty. It is a guarantee of periodic social transformation.

That hoped-for transformation, not periodic but in this case permanent, is what Jesus announces, when he begins with the statement: "The Spirit of the Lord God is upon me." Our role as Christian people and Christian churches is to serve as instruments of that transforma-tion. So we pray: "Spirit of Truth: Set us Free!"

Promise and judgment

When Jesus was reading the scripture (Luke 4:16-22) people in the synagogue were happy listening to the familiar verses. But they were astonished when Jesus said: "Today the scripture is fulfilled" (Luke 4:21).

Jesus had taken the text from Isaiah to its limits, making the words real, emphasizing God's special concern for the poor and marginalized. Jesus made it radically contem-poraneous. In the synagogue, however, the sense of surprise soon gave way to anger. This was scandalous, blasphemous. They wanted to do away with him!

This text is not only a promise but also a judgment, not only an affirmation of the poor, but also an invitation to the poor to establish justice, to rebuild places, cities, generations — and history. It is Good News, and it is judgment.

Nancy Pereira, Brazil

A call to be hopeful — and humble

"The Sovereign Lord has filled me with his Spirit." Who dare make such an affirmation? Only someone who is conscious of being sent with a particular mission in a specific context. Only Jesus of Nazareth makes this prophetic affirmation his own.

"The Sovereign Lord has filled me with his Spirit." He is upon me; he takes possession of me; I cannot escape him. He does not belong to me, but I belong to him. He sees me, he accompanies me; I am important for him, he takes me seriously. Is this really what we believe? Is it this assurance that motivates us? Do we live with this certainty?

The author of this text, perhaps an exile now back in his country, meets disillusionment everywhere. There is little enthusiasm. The construction of the temple drags on. The history of salvation seems to fail. Humanly speaking, this is a time of hopelessness. But facing this reality, in the face of intractable facts, the prophet stands up and says: "The Sovereign Lord has filled me with his Spirit." I don't speak in my name, I don't try to impose myself, but I have the conviction that what is now is not the last word! God will vindicate the humble ones, God will console the broken-hearted, God will liberate the captives. The ruins will be reconstructed, the rubble will be removed, the deserted town inhabited. A new future awaits us, and a fuller life.

It is with this conviction that Jesus began his ministry manifesting the presence of God among men and women. That is why he has been and is always "good news" to the people. Knowing this, the believers of today, at least in the West, should not lament over the state of the church, but they must put their confidence in the Spirit of strength and renewal, of creativity and change. Yes, we are invited to enter the ruins of our lives and our churches, and to live in them with the conviction that the Spirit of the Lord God is upon us, that the Spirit lives in us and in the world. This will make us humble and at the same time fill us with hope.

Michel Hoeffel, France

A village baptized

The year 1985 was the year of "the Lord's favour" for Liuliu Village in Choiseul Island of the Solomon Islands. Since September 1985 Liuliu village is called Loimuni.

For 38 years the people of Liuliu village had not been free. During those years they had been captivated by their human genealogies, wounded and broken by individualism, influenced by capitalism, blinded by economic development, oppressed by legalism. They were just caretakers of the outward form of religion!

During the week-end of 27-30 September 1985, I was invited to conduct a village-based conference (some of our people now call this type of conference "theological colleges in mobilized villages"). The subject of our Bible study was "Healing and sharing life in community".

On Sunday, 20 September 1985, at about 8 a.m. I began to feel the presence of the Spirit. At 10 o'clock in the morning I preached on the subject — "Let God transform you", based on Romans 12:1-2. The message was very simple and yet very powerful, the announcement of the message of the Lord's transforming power. At the end of my sermon, I made an appeal. Most of the people were standing up; they were not moving towards the front where I was standing, but moving towards their neighbours and enemies, embracing one another. They were weeping! We could not hear anything but singing and crying!

Their number one chief was crying and saying: "Do not cut and leave the stumps of the tree of our divided and broken community, but uproot it, before you leave us." So we worked hard for more than a day and night and we straightened out a number of things. From that time I discovered that when the court looked for *evidence* and our traditional customs looked for *compensation,* our forgiving and loving Father looked for *broken-heartedness.* The heart is the heart of any problem. If the Spirit of God is not permitted to break into our hearts then our religion is of no value.

Liuliu Village was baptized on 29 September 1985. It was given a new name, Loimuni: Lo — Love; Im — Immanuel; Uni — Unity.

Leslie Boseto, Solomon Islands

Questions for discussion

1. Facing situations of tyranny and oppression, we often tend to lose heart and hope. What is the message for us here? What does it mean in our local community to allow the Spirit of truth to set us free?

2. We have insisted on the social dimension of the prayer which is our theme for this study. We have affirmed that we are set free to serve. Where, and how, are we to witness to our freedom in the Spirit in specific acts of service?

3. Have we experiences of our own to share of the liberating work of the Spirit? Do we know of people who, led by the Spirit of truth, have been engaged in proclaiming "liberty to the captives"? What have they done? What are they doing now?

Almighty God,
you have broken the tyranny of sin
and have sent the Spirit of Truth into our hearts.

Give us grace to dedicate our freedom to your service,
that all creation may be brought
    to the glorious liberty of the children of God;
through Jesus Christ our Lord. Amen.

NOTES

BIBLE STUDY 5

Spirit of Unity — Reconcile your People!

O God, prosper the labours of all churches bearing the name of Christ and striving to further righteousness and faith in him. Help us to place your truth above our conception of it, and joyfully to recognize the presence of the Holy Spirit wherever the Spirit may choose to dwell. Teach us where we are sectarian in our intentions. Give us grace humbly to confess our fault to those whom in past days our communion had driven from its fellowship by ecclesiastical tyranny, spiritual barrenness or moral inefficiency. All this we ask so that we may become worthy and competent to bind up in the church the wounds of which we are guilty. We beseech you to hasten the day when there shall be one fold under one Shepherd, Jesus Christ our Lord. Amen.

Numbers 11:16-30
John 4:5-24

1 Corinthians 12:1-13:3

another—34 if any one is hungry, let him eat at home—lest you come together to be condemned. About the other things I will give directions when I come.

12 Now concerning spiritual gifts, brethren, I do not want you to be uninformed. 2 You know that when you were heathen, you were led astray to dumb idols, however you may have been moved. 3 Therefore I want you to understand that no one speaking by the Spirit of God ever says "Jesus be cursed!" and no one can say "Jesus is Lord" except by the Holy Spirit.

4 Now there are varieties of gifts, but the same Spirit; 5 and there are varieties of service, but the same Lord; 6 and there are varieties of working, but it is the same God who inspires them all in every one. 7 To each is given the manifestation of the Spirit for the common good. 8 To one is given through the Spirit the utterance of wisdom, and to another the utterance of knowledge according to the same Spirit, 9 to another faith by the same Spirit, to another gifts of healing by the one Spirit, 10 to another the working of miracles, to another prophecy, to another the ability to distinguish be-

tween spirits, to another various kinds of tongues, to another the interpretation of tongues. 11 All these are inspired by one and the same Spirit, who apportions to each one individually as he wills.

12 For just as the body is one and has many members, and all the members of the body, though many, are one body, so it is with Christ. 13 For by one Spirit we were all baptized into one body—Jews or Greeks, slaves or free—and all were made to drink of one Spirit.

14 For the body does not consist of one member but of many. 15 If the foot should say, "Because I am not a hand, I do not belong to the body," that would not make it any less a part of the body. 16 And if the ear should say, "Because I am not an eye, I do not belong to the body," that would not make it any less a part of the body. 17 If the whole body were an eye, where would be the hearing? If the whole body were an ear, where would be the sense of smell? 18 But as it is, God arranged the organs in the body, each one of them, as he chose. 19 If all were a single organ, where would the body be? 20 As it is, there are many parts, yet one body. 21 The eye cannot say to the hand, "I have no need of you," nor again the head to the feet, "I have no need of you." 22 On the contrary, the parts of the body which seem to be weaker are indispensable, 23 and those parts of the body which we think less honourable we invest with the greater honour, and our unpresentable parts are treated with greater modesty, 24 which our more presentable parts do not require. But God has so adjusted the body, giving the greater honour to the inferior part, 25 that there may be no discord in the body, but that the members may have the same care for one another. 26 If one member suffers, all suffer together; if one member is honoured, all rejoice together.

27 Now you are the body of Christ and individually members of it. 28 And God has appointed in the church first apostles, second prophets, third teachers, then workers of miracles, then healers, helpers, administrators, speakers in various kinds of tongues. 29 Are all apostles? Are all prophets? Are all teachers? Do all work miracles? 30 Do all possess gifts of healing? Do all speak with tongues? Do all interpret? 31 But earnestly desire the higher gifts.

And I will show you a still more excellent way.

13 If I speak in the tongues of men and of angels, but have not love, I am a noisy gong or a clanging cymbal. 2 And if I have prophetic powers, and understand all mysteries and all knowledge, and if I have all faith, so as to remove mountains, but have not love, I am nothing. 3 If I give away all I have, and if I deliver my body to be burned,*v* but have not love, I gain nothing.

4 Love is patient and kind; love is not jealous or boastful; 5 it is not arrogant or

---

To reconcile is to restore relationships. In the Old Testament "reconciliation" has to do chiefly with the restoration of Israel's relationship with God. In the New Testament it also signifies the restoration of human relationships. Paul's statement that "in Christ God was reconciling the world to himself" (**2 Cor. 5:19**; see also **Col. 1:20**) extends the scope of reconciliation to the whole world.

It is the Spirit who enables us to appropriate this cosmic reconciliation, for "no one can say 'Jesus is Lord' except by the Holy Spirit" (**v.3b**). The lordship of Christ is not a human discovery; it is a confession of faith to which the Spirit leads us. It is through the Holy Spirit working in us that we are restored to communion with God and community with people.

The main passage chosen for our study is from Paul's (first) letter to Corinthian Christians. Corinth, the capital of a Roman province, was a thriving cosmopolitan city. It was a centre of commerce, with a population that was intellectually active but morally corrupt. Paul had spent over 18 months in the city, "teaching the word of God", and he left behind him a strong church, composed mostly of poor people. But now Paul hears from various sources of serious problems in the Corinthian church — cases of gross immorality, idolatrous practices, factions and parties, quarrelling and dissension. These are the issues he addresses in the letter.

In the passage we are studying, Paul's chief concern is with the unity of the church. But the very gifts of the Spirit have resulted in divisions. They are valued for themselves, without reference to what they are meant for, the upbuilding of the community. In that process people have developed their own hierarchy of gifts, the more spectacular ones predictably taking the top places.

Paul affirms that all these gifts are gifts of the Spirit, but they are all for the benefit of the community and their usefulness can be determined only in terms of how far they contribute to the wellbeing of the community. Using that criterion, he sees, for example, the gift of prophecy as of greater value than the gift of tongues. But what is more important than even prophecy is the practice of love, without which the purpose for which the gifts are given cannot be realized. **Chapter 13** is a hymn in praise of love. It is not a digression, but central to Paul's argument which he continues in the following chapter.

Paul takes the illustration from the human body to its logical limits. That the parts or *members* of the body need each other is obvious. Paul's point is that in themselves the individual parts or functions have no value whatever. It is not that the gifts exercised by the members complement or enrich one another, which of course they should. Paul wants to make it absolutely clear that these gifts are worthless unless they become an integrated part of the total ministry of the community of faith. Any spiritual gift has value — indeed can be recognized as spiritual — only insofar as it has a place in the "body".

The Spirit of unity, therefore, "holds the body together", providing the dynamism of true mutuality and co-working. Reconciliation is the process through which a person or a group — led to a new relationship with God and neighbours — becomes part of the "body" instead of a "somebody" in him- or herself.

There is indeed a variety of gifts, but there is only one Spirit. There are indeed different ways of serving, but there is only one Lord. The oneness of the One whom we serve is the basis of our unity. Early in **1 Corinthians** Paul wrote: "What I mean is that each one of you says, 'I belong to Paul', or 'I belong to Apollos', or 'I belong to Cephas' or 'I belong to Christ'. Is Christ divided? Was Paul crucified for you? Or were you baptized in the name of Paul?" **(1:12,13)**. It will be an interesting exercise to paraphrase these verses in terms of the church divisions in our own localities.

In many of our churches "extraordinary charismata", spiritual gifts that often attract popular attention, tend to be overvalued, as they were in the church in Corinth. Paul provides a new perspective for the appreciation of the gifts of the Spirit. We saw in our first study how the Spirit of God often speaks to us in "a still small voice". Our response to the Spirit can also be through quiet acts and words of love.

The Spirit creates unity and helps us to share responsibility in a variety of ways. Moses was guided by God's Spirit. In the story from Numbers we see God giving the same Spirit to the seventy elders, in order to serve the unity and welfare of the whole community. But the manifestation of the Spirit is not confined to the holy places. In the camps "outside the camp" (cf. **Heb. 13:12**) also the Spirit is at work. Joshua is understandably jealous. He would rather own and control the Spirit. But Moses is generous and open-minded. "Would that all the Lord's people were prophets, that the Lord would put his Spirit upon them!" **(v.29)**. How often we, like Joshua, claim complete monopoly for all the gifts of the Spirit!

Much has been said and written in recent years about Jesus' encounter with the woman of Samaria. Our concern in the passage we are studying is to highlight the teaching that the Spirit of God is not confined to Mount Gerizim in Samaria or Mount Zion in Jerusalem. Recall the story of the conversion of Cornelius in **Acts 10.** It involved the conversion of Peter as well. He learned, not without difficulty, that God has no favourites. God's Spirit acts in freedom, truth and love — with men and women, people of all races and social backgrounds. There is an ecumenical insight in the account of Jesus' meeting with the Samaritan woman which can inform and deepen our reflections on reconciliation.

"Our eyes were opened"

The body of Christ — the church
"Mother Church" I heard them call it
but she had a male body and a male face —
apostles, prophets, teachers,
the priests at the altars.

I was taught that only a man
can represent Christ —
for he was a man —
"God became man".

I was taught that God arranged
the organs in the body as he chose
and each has a different gift
according to God's grace.

I was taught that love
is the special gift entrusted to women
and that love is patient and kind,
that love is not jealous or boastful,
arrogant or rude;
that love does not insist on its own way,
that love bears and endures all things.

I was taught that my body
has less honourable and unpresentable parts;
that, therefore, I am not pure enough
to touch the body of Christ;

that, because of the blood flowing from my body,
I am not permitted
to touch the cup filled with the blood of Christ.

One day I woke up and went out
to find my sisters — and we realized:
when one member suffers, all suffer together —
sharing our tears and deep wounds,
our buried hopes and longings,
we looked at each other and saw
the image of God.
And suddenly we felt a gentle breeze
and heard a voice saying:
"Do you not know that your bodies
are members of Christ
and temples in which I am dwelling?"
And she added: "Never forget!
You were all baptized into Christ.
So there is neither Jew nor Greek,
neither slave nor free,
neither male nor female;
for you are all one in Christ Jesus."

Our eyes were opened
and we felt our hearts burning.
And we rose that same hour
and returned to our brothers.

Ingrid R. Kitzberger, FRG

The call to "run and embrace" all people

"It is a terrible, an inexorable, law that one cannot deny
the humanity of another without diminishing one's own,"
writes James Baldwin of Harlem in New York City. "I am
because we are, and since we are therefore I am," says
the Ugandan theologian John S. Mbiti. When we live
contrary to the truth of human inter-relatedness and
mutuality we are "led astray to dumb idols". Idols
(emperor worship of all kinds accompanied by all kinds of
music; see Dan. 3:5-7) destroy human inter-relatedness
and human community. Martin Luther King wrote from
the Birmingham City Jail (1963): "Any law that uplifts
human personality is just. Any law that degrades human

personality is unjust." The varieties of gifts that come from the Spirit uplift the quality of our personal, communal, national, international and cosmic life. They speak critical and awakened words. They are against idolatry. The Spirit, through them, works to create "the shape of Christ" (Gal. 4:19) in us and in our world.

The shape of Christ is portrayed in the image of the body of Christ. The church as the body of Christ is bound up with the image of the body of Christ broken "for you" in the Last Supper (1 Cor. 11:23-26). Christ's "brokenness" is his self-giving openness to the whole creation. "But while he was yet at a distance, his father saw him and had compassion and ran and embraced him and kissed him" (Luke 15:20). The church, the body of the "broken" Christ, must "run and embrace" all peoples. Not the image of Noah's Ark but that of the waiting father running out to receive the returning son (Luke 15:20) must be the central image that nurtures Christian life. Christ who eats "with sinners and tax collectors" (Mark 2:16) — in such a simple act of sharing — intimates the love which goes beyond "all mysteries and all knowledge".

Kosuke Koyama, Japan/USA

The birth of democracy

My comment is based on the Numbers passage. I see in it the beginnings of democracy. Moses, it would appear, was not very good at delegating authority. He was God's own choice, and he was all too conscious of it. Though reluctant at first, he grew into a powerful leader and jealous of his power and prerogatives. In this he was ably assisted by loyalists like Joshua.

Now God asks Moses to call all the elders of Israel and gather them around the Tent of Meeting. God wants to demonstrate that leadership needs to be a shared responsibility. On the morrow all but two of the elders come together. Eldad and Medad have decided to stay behind. They must have said to themselves: "It is futile to go to these meetings. Nothing will be changed. The old man cannot really delegate power. So why bother? From time

76

to time he likes putting up these shows, but it will be business as usual in no time!"

Suddenly, however, things are different. God has openly and visibly distributed the Spirit that was upon Moses to the elders, to Eldad and Medad as well as to those gathered around the Tent of Meeting. Under the sway of the Spirit all are given ecstatic utterance as a visible sign of God's accepting them as co-leaders with Moses.

Now Joshua is greatly disturbed because his leader Moses is no longer the unique one. Further, the defiant Eldad and Medad are also recognized by God. Surely, this cannot be allowed! There must be something wrong. So he runs to Moses and reports that Eldad and Medad, the two who had all along questioned Moses' way of doing things, were also prophesying. Moses must stop them, he urges.

Thank God, by this time Moses has learnt his lesson. He has learnt that it is God's will that leadership must be a corporate affair. He has also learnt to discern the ills arising out of listening to over-enthusiastic loyalists such as Joshua. So he now rebukes Joshua, saying: "Are you jealous for me? Would to God that all were God's prophets."

Would to God that God will win everywhere where leaders thrive on hero worship and make people their slaves!
Dayanchand Carr, India

A personal testimony

Like many others, I became serious about Jesus Christ in my college years. I committed my life to him and after seminary training set out to serve God through a para-church agency.

A group of us began studying 1 Corinthians 12-14 (and John 17 and Ephesians 4). We would ask ourselves: "Where is this unity today?" Apparently there are over 2,600 denominations and Christian "groups" in America. How does one go about restoring Christian unity?

After resigning from our para-church organization, we called together other pastoral types from around the country who were interested in finding or building a model of New Testament community. Without meaning to, we ended up with people from a huge variety of Christian backgrounds. Our goal was to experience the New Testament church, to serve the Lord and each other, and to operate by consensus — much the same way as did the early church councils. Though diversified as to our spiritual gifts and ministries, and while far from perfect, we entered into a common journey of Christ-centred faith, worship and sacramental life.

Our journey together was fulfilled with a new beginning. In 1987, this group of people, about 2,000 strong, was

received *en masse* into the Orthodox Church. If God could bring *us* together, we believe he can heal the ancient schisms among all Christians.

Peter E. Gillquist, USA

Understanding love as political and spiritual power

"On the contrary, the parts of the body which seem to be weaker are indispensable." While this chapter has been interpreted to affirm the contribution of each part to an integrated whole, the church has made little effort to affirm the fact that "the weaker parts are indispensable", and that a new community in Jesus Christ can be viewed only from the perspective of those on the underside of history.

In fact this passage has often been quoted to encourage women and all oppressed people to be satisfied with the role they have been assigned by a hierarchical, patriarchal church and society. But verse 12 says only that some parts of the body (the community) "*seem* to be weaker". That is, they *think* they are weak, because they are taught to believe they are *and* to accept their position as their "God-ordained" lot. Centuries of colonial, neo-colonial and imperialist domination, with the connivance of caste, class and racial power groups within colonized nations, have undermined the experiences, the contributions and value of large sections of the population — taking away from them their dignity and self-worth.

But a new wind blows over the world, as dominated people recognize that they "are indispensable", that they only "seem" to be weaker parts of the body. This consciousness has led to an eruption all over the globe with people reclaiming their power, their right to belong as co-heirs to all the beauty and the resources of creation.

They have given to 1 Corinthians 13 a new vitality — love is political and spiritual power — the power to have faith in a new order where all of creation will live with justice, in peace and integrity. These too are the gifts of the Holy

79

Spirit and have to be appropriated by those who "seem weak" if they are to be accepted as an indispensable part of the whole.

Aruna Gnanadason, India

Questions for discussion

1. Can you identify the gifts of the Spirit in your congregation and church? Are all of them equally valued? Where do you see the Holy Spirit working outside Christian circles?

2. What is your comment on the following experience of a Scandinavian Christian? "Some years ago I was invited to attend a training programme for glossolalia, speaking in tongues, in the Holy Land. I thought it was impossible, because speaking in tongues in the biblical sense is a gift, isn't it? Can it be the result of a training programme? But I participated. It was a very enthusiastic fellowship — nice atmosphere, good teachers, fine music — and it was not too expensive for those who could not learn it within five days. And I could not! In the eyes of the others I was after that no more a Christian, so they cut contacts with me, because they thought I was lacking a clear sign of true faith..."

3. How do confessional and denominational divisions arise, and how are they perpetuated? At what points and in what ways do you feel called to exercise the ministry of reconciliation in your context — religious, social, political and economic?

Coming down and confusing the tongues, the Most High divided the nations; but distributing the tongues of fire, the Most High called all to unity. Therefore, with one voice, we glorify the all-holy Spirit!

NOTES

BIBLE STUDY 6

Holy Spirit — Transform and Sanctify Us!

O heavenly King,
Comforter,
the Spirit of Truth,
present in all places and filling all things,
treasury of good things and giver of life,
come and dwell in us
and purify us from every stain,
and of your goodness save our souls.
Amen.

Ezekiel 37:1-14
1 John 4:1-16

Mark 1:4-13

1 The beginning of the gospel of Jesus Christ, the Son of God.[a]

2 As it is written in Isaiah the prophet,[b]

"Behold, I send my messenger before thy face,
who shall prepare thy way;
3 the voice of one crying in the wilderness:
Prepare the way of the Lord,
make his paths straight—"

4 John the baptizer appeared[c] in the wilderness, preaching a baptism of repentance for the forgiveness of sins. 5 And there went out to him all the country of Judea, and all the people of Jerusalem; and they were baptized by him in the river Jordan, confessing their sins. 6 Now John was clothed with camel's hair, and had a leather girdle around his waist, and ate locusts and wild honey. 7 And he preached, saying, "After me comes he who is mightier than I, the thong of whose sandals I am not worthy to stoop down and untie. 8 I have baptized you with water; but he will baptize you with the Holy Spirit."

9 In those days Jesus came from Nazareth of Galilee and was baptized by John in the Jordan. 10 And when he came up out of the water, immediately he saw the heavens opened and the Spirit descending upon him like a dove; 11 and a voice came from heaven, "Thou art my beloved Son;[d] with thee I am well pleased."

12 The Spirit immediately drove him out into the wilderness. 13 And he was in the wilderness forty days, tempted by Satan; and he was with the wild beasts; and the angels ministered to him.

14 Now after John was arrested, Jesus

The prophecy of Ezekiel, like that of Jeremiah, is about pulling down and building up. Its theme is judgment and mercy, destruction and restoration. The God who scatters also gathers; the God who destroys also restores.

The dry bones symbolize Israel. A people in exile, they have lost their country, their temple and their history. Humanly speaking Israel has no future. They are reduced to bones, and the bones are "very dry".

In Ezekiel's vision, the restoration takes place in two stages. He prophesies to the bones, and conveys to them "the word of the Lord" **(vv.4-8)**. But that results only in a partial restoration. There are whole bodies now, but there is no life in them. God asks Ezekiel to call upon the Spirit, the life-giving breath; when he does, the bodies not only live but stand upon their own feet **(vv.9,10)**. The resurrection that takes place is not only of persons but of a community, "an exceedingly great host". The message is clear: "And I will put my Spirit within you, and you shall live" **(v.14)**. Live, not only as isolated individuals, but as a transformed community.

The prophet's vision is one of transformation. To transform is to change the form as well as the substance and the character. In New Testament terms it is to put off the old nature and put on "the new nature" **(Col. 3:9,10)**. It is to become "a new creation" **(Gal. 6:15)**.

To sanctify is to make holy. "You shall be holy," the Lord wanted Moses to say to the people of Israel, "for I the Lord your God am holy" **(Lev. 19:2;** see **1 Pet. 1:10-16)**. But we cannot on our own put off our old nature or put on the new nature. We cannot on our own become holy. The Holy Spirit alone can transform and sanctify us.

The *New* Testament bears witness to the *new* covenant that God has made with us in Christ Jesus. We are made new, transformed and sanctified, through our acceptance of the new covenant, and it is the Spirit who makes it possible.

The baptism of Jesus marks a crucial stage in the new covenant God has made with us. Jesus inaugurates the new creation, and it is significant that Mark begins his account of our Lord's earthly ministry with the story of his baptism. Immersion was a traditional rite of purification in ancient religions. The baptism of John was an expression of repentance and a sign of moral purification. Jesus probably accepts it as an act of solidarity with his people, a vicarious confession of sin, in order to fulfill all that the saving righteousness of God demands (see **Matt. 3:15**). It denotes thus the beginning of the new dispensation, the messianic era.

The Spirit who hovered over the waters at creation "in the beginning" now descends on Jesus "like a dove" at the beginning of the new creation. And a voice speaks from heaven, God's own word, affirming the person and mission of Jesus. The verses we are studying have been rightly described as one of the great Trinitarian passages in the Bible.

Jesus is seen, to use a familiar expression, as the "new Adam"; he ushers in the new order and is its first fruits (**1 Cor. 15:20-23**). Through his baptism he both inaugurated and participated in life in the new dispensation. No wonder baptism, in the history of the church, is closely related to new creation, to transformation and sanctification, marking as it does our entry into the community of faith, the Spirit-empowered body of Christ.

The Holy Spirit anointed Jesus for his ministry. He is now the Christ of God, the Anointed One. According to the church fathers the Spirit also sanctified the water so that all who go through the baptismal water may be made holy.

We began this series of biblical reflections by confessing, in the words of the Nicene Creed, our faith in the Holy Spirit. We then called upon the Spirit on behalf of the whole creation, praying that it may be renewed. Affirming the Spirit as the source of all life, we prayed that all creation may be sustained. The sole revealer of truth, the Spirit alone can set us free, and we prayed that we may be set free to serve and love. Unity and community are the gifts of the Holy Spirit, and we prayed that we may be reconciled to God and to people. And now we beseech the Spirit to transform and sanctify us. But how do we discern the Spirit? How do we distinguish between the Holy Spirit who is the Giver of Life and the spirits that diminish and corrupt human life? We read in **Mark 1** that, after Jesus' baptism, the Spirit "drove him out into the wilderness" **(v.12)**. A few verses later we read of Jesus rebuking "an unclean spirit" **(vv.23-26)**. How indeed do we distinguish between the Holy Spirit and the unclean or evil spirits?

John addresses that important question of how to "test the spirits" in the passage we are studying. In general John's letters are of a pastoral nature. His concern is to establish Christian people in their faith in Christ. But here he warns them against the "many false prophets", "the spirit of antichrist" and "the spirit of error".

John's criterion of discernment is this: "Every spirit which confesses that Jesus Christ has come in the flesh is of God" **(v.2)**. The Holy Spirit alone enables us to make that confession. Like every other confession of faith this is also a commitment of life, with a deep social significance. It enables us to love one another. We must love one another, says John, not only because love is of the essence of God (God is love: **v.8**) but also because the love of God was supremely manifested in history in the self-giving love of the Son of God **(v.10)**, and because in the act of loving one another we show forth the love of God **(v.12)**.

It is the Holy Spirit who, by transforming and sanctifying us, enables us to love one another. Our life in community, serving and loving one another, in turn witnesses to the presence of the Spirit in our churches, our communities, and our own lives.

Jesus Christ is God's gift to us. He is what is *new*; in him we see the scope and goal of God's renewing work. The Holy Spirit who opens our eyes to see this new reality also enables us to be involved, with Christ and in the manner of Christ, in that renewing work. Our prayer is also an act of dedication.

87

The desert, the Spirit and the baptism

In the gospel passages and sermons in our Western society we frequently describe the historical Jesus as a busy preacher, healer and activist. By doing so we make him in our imagination a superman, and hence a captive of our present-day culture and historical situation.

The Christian tradition, however, also knows another Jesus, the spiritual relative of John the Baptist. He was a human person who led a simple life, and often retired to solitude in order to fast, pray and be silent.

In solitude Jesus fought against the demons and evil spirits. Many great ascetics in the history of the church have been called to follow the same vocation. This has been and still is a tried and tested path to mental and spiritual growth.

The forty days that Jesus spent in the wilderness in preparation for his public life and service cannot be taken too literally. They are more likely to be an Old Testament typology, referring to his long inner struggle and growth which might have taken years, even decades.

John the fore-runner and Jesus himself belong to that group of God's people who, to a great extent, lived and worked outside organized society. Under the guidance of the Spirit they were led to their suffering, to carrying their crosses. The dying of "the bare grain" was the beginning of a great project.

The desert, the Spirit and the baptism always belong together. Whilst taking the baptismal oaths Christians commit themselves to renouncing the world, its vanity, its pride and pomp, and even their natural worldly bonds. Instead, at baptism we give a solemn vow of obedience to Christ the King. This is the beginning of a life-long process of transformation and sanctification. It is a dialogue with Christ taking place in the Spirit, and it will lead towards the likeness of the prototype provided by Christ.

Ambrosios, Finland

The meaning of baptism

This text reminds me of a profound spiritual and ethical dimension in baptism — John's, Jesus' and ours. Baptism as a sacrament is an act in the presence of God whose love is a holy love which does not permit an easy by-passing of divine judgment. It unites us with Jesus, the Christ, about whom this Gospel story tells me a great deal. And it carries with it the promise of the Spirit without whose strength I cannot cope with the difficulties and opportunities of life.

The scripture tells me that — as my baptism took place "into Christ" — I am involved in the story of this man Jesus of Nazareth, in a movement of God's Spirit which is marked by the temptations and victories of Jesus, and, finally, that I need to be involved in the spreading of the Good News coming from God if I am committed to live a life which matches the challenge of my baptism.

Günter Wagner, Switzerland

Shaking us up

At the time of his baptism, according to the account in Mark 1:4-13, Jesus experienced God the Holy Spirit in two different ways. He saw the Spirit coming towards him like a dove — to give him comforting affirmation of God's favour towards him. He immediately (how Mark loves that word!) felt the same Spirit driving him out into an uncomfortable place for a period of spiritual struggle.

In our own encounters with God the Spirit, I believe, we meet both of those dimensions of God's holiness in action. God invites us to closer relationship, stretches out God's arms and welcomes us, even runs down the road to meet us. Yet God does not tuck us into bed and pull a cosy blanket up under our chins, as if we were children. Because we too are responsible adults, God the Spirit disturbs our complacency, challenges our false securities, pushes us out into unfamiliar and sometimes frightening times and places.

Throughout his ministry, from his baptism to the cross, Jesus knew God's Spirit at work in his life in both ways. On the basis of my own experience, I find that when I am willing to let God shake me up (I call that God "Holy Dynamite"), I am better able to feel God's arm around my shoulders also as friend and counsellor.

Marianne H. Micks, USA

No guarantee against temptation

The setting is very pictorial, the drama very graphic. Two movements from opposite directions intersect and then diverge again in opposite directions. John the preacher comes in from the wilderness, baptizes at the River Jordan and then disappears into Herod's prison (1:4-5,9,14). Jesus the Nazarene comes from the town, is baptized by John in the River Jordan and then goes off into the wilderness (1:9,12).

The point of intersection is the place of revelation and supernatural empowerment. He of whom the preacher could only speak anonymously as the Mightier One, and who, up to that point, was known only as Jesus of Nazareth (1:7-9), is there acclaimed, manifested and endowed as the Beloved Son (1:11), the Anointed One (1:1).

No such dignity or endowment has been bestowed on John. There is nothing messianic about him. No pronouncement has been made over him. He is merely the messenger, a voice crying in the wilderness, preaching and administering a baptism of repentance (1:2-5). He is like a meteor coming suddenly into view, which is very conspicuous for a little while, and then disappears, never to be seen or heard of again. Jesus, on the other hand, is driven by the Spirit into the wilderness for a forty-day ordeal which is a necessary preparation for, and a foretaste of, the ministry which is about to commence.

The thrust is therefore clear. The two movements represented by these two figures are set in a contrasting relationship. They are qualitatively different. There is no natural continuity from the one to the other — not even through the baptism, because it is only *after* the baptism is over that the dove is seen and the voice is heard.

In Mark, as in the Fourth Gospel, John the Baptist is the counterfoil of Jesus. Where the one is diminished the other is increased, where the one ends the other begins. John is not the Light (John 1:8). Though first in time, he does not enjoy the precedence (John 1:15). He is neither Messiah nor Elijah, nor even a prophet, but only a voice (John 1:19-23). He can work no miracles, but only bear a faithful witness to the Christ (John 10:41; 1:8). He must therefore decrease as Jesus increases (John 3:30).

Therefore John is spared the ordeal of the Mightier One, he is not Satan's target. The wilderness is for him a monastery, not a place of trial and peril. It is the Mightier One, acclaimed, empowered and propelled by the Spirit who becomes exposed to temptation, and who moves between ministering angels and wild beasts.

The passage therefore leaves us with this very salutary and sobering thought. The Holy Spirit is no guarantee against temptation. On the contrary, the very powers the Spirit bestows carry their own special dangers and temptations. The angels who wait to serve and the wild beasts who threaten to undo and undermine are never very far from the Spirit-filled and Spirit-led.

William Watty, Trinidad

A prayer to the Holy Trinity

In the desert of our petrified souls, without shade or water, appears John the Baptist, calling upon us to repent, and to look upon the Lamb of God who carries our sins. Then the Lord appears, sanctified by the Father's Spirit and blessed by his voice. Let us worship the Holy Trinity for the salvation that Christ brings to us.

Holy Father, you called us out of the desert of our sins to share in your everlasting kingdom. Help us by the power of your Spirit to live in your presence.

Holy Son, you have by your humility blessed the waters of Jordan; bless our life, and send your Holy Spirit to abide with us and renew us from within.

Holy Spirit, purify our bodies, sanctify us, and make us a temple where you will be permanently present.

Holy Trinity, bless our coming together in your name. Deliever us from the evil one, lead us into your truth and renew in us the image and likeness of your being, for you are both the source and goal of our life. Amen.

Qais Sadiq, Lebanon

The call to speak out

The problems facing the churches in the South Pacific today are the oppressive effects of transnational corporations, nuclear testing and their ecological effects, militarization of the region and the struggle for political independence and self-determination. What should concern them most is the living of the Gospel today.

It is difficult to understand why the churches continue to remain silent in the midst of these injustices. Two reasons may be given: lack of information, and a conservative and fundamentalist theology.

John the Baptist's call for repentance speaks strongly to the churches in the South Pacific today. We need to change our ways of doing things. We need conversion in our theological orientation, to stop reducing the gospel to personal salvation, and set it free to serve the good of people: the suffering, the sick and blind, the lonely, confused, poor and oppressed, and the ignorant. We need the transforming and sanctifying power of the Holy Spirit that Jesus gives to the church.

Isn't it true that if the church, like Jesus, committed itself whole-heartedly to the purposes of God — to love and care for the wellbeing of all people and the whole creation — its thinking will become alert, alternatives and possibilities will slip into focus, and temptations will become stronger and also clearer?

Puafitu Faa'alo, Tuvalu

Questions for discussion

1. At baptism we receive the Holy Spirit; we are admitted to the community of faith and we become heirs of a hope for today and for hereafter. But baptism has also ethical and social implications. Is this our understanding of baptism? How far is all this evident in our life together?

2. Prophecy is a gift of the Holy Spirit. The prophet is the mouthpiece of the Spirit. But there is the Spirit, *and* there are spirits, prophets *and* prophets. How do we distinguish between the true prophet and the false?

3. How can we become:

   a) More receptive to God's gift of the Spirit?

   b) More open to the work of the Spirit outside our community of faith?

   c) More responsible for God's creation, for justice and peace in all human relations and for the stewardship of the world?

Holy Spirit, Creator,
at the beginning you hovered over the waters;
you breathed life into all creatures;
without you every living creature dies and returns to nothingness,
Come into us, Holy Spirit.

Holy Spirit, Comforter,
by you we are born again as children of God;
you make us living temples of your presence,
you pray within us with prayers too deep for words,
Come into us, Holy Spirit.

Holy Spirit, Lord and Giver of Life,
you are light, you bring us light;
you are goodness and the source of all goodness,
Come into us, Holy Spirit.

Holy Spirit, Breath of Life,
you sanctify and breathe life into the whole body of the church;
you dwell in each one of its members,
and will one day give new life to our mortal bodies,
Come into us, Holy Spirit.

NOTES

Sources and Acknowledgments

The scripture quotations in this publication are from the Revised Standard Version of the Bible, copyrighted 1971 and 1952 by the Division of Christian Education of the National Council of the Churches of Christ in the USA.

Page 16: *Blessed Lord, you speak to us*, reprinted from the Lutheran Book of Worship, © 1978, by permission of Augsburg Fortress.

Page 24: *Almighty God, who on the day of Pentecost*, The Alternative Service Book 1980, p.635, © The Central Board of Finance of the Church of England 1980, London, UK.

Page 28: *O God, the Holy Spirit, come to us, and among us*, from "My God My Glory", by Eric Milner-White, SPCK, London, UK.

Page 38: *O God, life-giving Spirit*, Movement for the ordination of women, Great Britain.

Page 42: *We praise you, Holy Spirit, our Advocate and Comforter*, WCC-Commission on the Churches' Participation in Development, Newsletter, January 1982, adapted.

Page 54: *O Great Spirit, whose breath gives life to the world*, Report of the Hymnal Revision Committee to the 1988 General Conference of the United Methodist Church, USA, United Methodist Publishing House, Nashville, USA.

Page 58: *The wind of the Spirit challenges us to change*, Dorothy McMahon, Pitt Street Parish of the Uniting Church in Australia, Sydney, Australia.

Page 66: *Almighty God, you have broken the tyranny of sin*, The Alternative Service Book 1980, p.653, © The Central Board of Finance of the Church of England 1980, London, UK.

Page 70: *O God, prosper the labours of all churches*, by Bishop Brent of the USA, 1862-1929.

Page 80: *Coming down and confusing the tongues*, Orthodox hymn.

Page 84: *O heavenly King, Comforter*, Orthodox prayer.

Page 94: *Holy Spirit, Creator*, © Ateliers et Presses de Taizé, 71250 Cluny, France.

Photos

Pages 14, 26, 31, 36, 40, 48, 56, 65, 68, 82: WCC/Peter Williams
Page 5: WCC
Page 21: Sebastiao Salgado
Page 52: United Methodist Missions/Toge Fujihira
Page 78: WCC/John Taylor
Page 89: EDP/Fechter

NOTES

NOTES

NOTES

NOTES